Shostakovich Symphonies and Concertos

Unlocking the Masters Series, No. 9

Series Editor: Robert Levine

Shostakovich Symphonies and Concertos

An Owner's Manual

David Hurwitz

AMADEUS PRESS

Copyright © 2006 by David Hurwitz
All rights reserved. No part of this book may be reproduced in any form, without written permission, except by a newspaper or magazine reviewer who wishes to quote brief passages in connection with a review.

Published in 2006 by Amadeus Press, LLC
512 Newark Pompton Turnpike, Pompton Plains, New Jersey 07444, USA
Website: www.amadeuspress.com

The poem "A Career" by Yevgeny Yevtuchenko in Symphony No. 13 is reprinted by permission of G. Schirmer, Inc. The English translation is by David Hurwitz.

For the quotation of the passage from *Galina: A Russian Story* by Galina Vishnevskaya, gratitude is expressed to Harcourt Brace Jovanovich.

While every effort has been made to trace copyright holders and obtain permission, this has not been possible in all cases; any omissions brought to our attention will be remedied in future editions.

Book design by Clare Cerullo

Printed in the United States of America

Library of Congress Cataloging-in-Publication Data is available upon request.

ISBN 1-57467-131-6

To my dear friends, Claire and Christophe, with fondest hopes that their life together utterly lacks the drama of a Shostakovich symphony!

Contents

Part 1: Shostakovich's Musical Language

THE SHOSTAKOVICH QUESTION	3
LISTENING TO SHOSTAKOVICH	17
SYMPHONY NO. 5 *1937*	21

Part 2: Early-Period Works

SYMPHONY NO. 1 *1924–25*	37
SYMPHONY NO. 2 ("TO OCTOBER") *1927*	45
SYMPHONY NO. 3 ("THE FIRST OF MAY") *1929*	49
PIANO CONCERTO NO. 1 *1933*	53

Part 3: Middle-Period Works

SYMPHONY NO. 4 *1935–36*	61
SYMPHONY NO. 6 *1939*	73
SYMPHONY NO. 7 ("LENINGRAD") *1941*	81
SYMPHONY NO. 8 *1943*	95
SYMPHONY NO. 9 *1945*	107
VIOLIN CONCERTO NO. 1 *1947–48, revised 1955*	113
SYMPHONY NO. 10 *1953*	123

Part 4: Late-Period Works

SYMPHONY NO. 11 ("THE YEAR 1905") *1957*	137
PIANO CONCERTO NO. 2 *1957*	147
CELLO CONCERTO NO. 1 *1959*	151
SYMPHONY NO. 12 ("THE YEAR 1917") *1961*	157
SYMPHONY NO. 13 ("BABI YAR") *1962*	167
CELLO CONCERTO NO. 2 *1966*	181
VIOLIN CONCERTO NO. 2 *1967*	189
SYMPHONY NO. 14 *1969*	193
SYMPHONY NO. 15 *1971*	201
POSTLUDE	209
APPENDIX 1: CHRONOLOGY OF WORKS	213
APPENDIX 2: SUMMARY OF INDIVIDUAL MOVEMENT FORMS	219
SELECTED BIBLIOGRAPHY	221
CD TRACK LISTING	223

Part 1

Shostakovich's Musical Language

The Shostakovich Question

All intensely expressive music that does not purport to tell a story or make obvious reference to anything beyond basic human emotions—including most of the symphonies and concertos of Dmitri Shostakovich (1906–75)—naturally begs the question of what it is that the composer is trying to say. The case of Shostakovich presents this problem in a particularly acute form. So much so, in fact, that an entire field of academia has been created in order to attempt to ferret out any biographical or programmatic subtexts concealed in his major works. That such hidden meanings exist is beyond question. The composer himself suggested as much. However, the degree to which his verbal statements can be believed and the accuracy with which they have been transmitted remains an object of great controversy embodied in numerous books and articles, and much very real (if often entertaining) hostility among scholars and researchers.

The study of Shostakovich's life is indeed a fascinating subject, perhaps the seminal opportunity to examine the complex relationship between artistic genius and the cultural policies of an evil, totalitarian regime. Exactly how the music fits into this equation is a puzzle that resists easy solution. After all, the entire point of hidden meanings is that they remain hidden. Shostakovich is gone, taking his secrets with him to the grave.

Those of his friends who were privy to his private thoughts (or who claim that they were) have spoken. The sum total of what they have to say, however interesting or moving biographically, not only has turned out to be largely unenlightening as an aid to understanding his music as such, but it pales beside the elemental power and eloquence of the various works themselves.

I can think of only one major exception to the above generalization among accounts of the composer available in English, written by those who actually knew him well, and this is the portrait of Shostakovich offered by Galina Vishnevskaya, the greatest Russian soprano of the twentieth century and wife of the world-famous cellist/conductor Mstislav Rostropovich. Her autobiography, *Galina: A Russian Story* remains arguably the finest personal memoir of artistic life under the Soviet regime, and her summary and description of the "Shostakovich question" is so succinctly compelling and complete, so useful in establishing the context for the following discussion of the music itself, that it deserves to be quoted at length.

Vishnevskaya picks up the story in 1935, when the composer was twenty-nine and basking in the success of his opera *Lady Macbeth of Mtsensk*:

> Dmitri Shostakovich was ascending the very heights of fame—young, brilliant, and recognized not only in Russia but throughout the world. His First Symphony, written when he was only nineteen, had, by the time he was twenty, crossed the Soviet borders to be performed by the best orchestras under the greatest conductors: Arturo Toscanini, Bruno Walter, Leopold Stokowski, Serge Koussevitsky. And during those fateful years especially, his music was performed often in America. In addition to his symphonies, *Lady Macbeth* premiered in New York at the Metropolitan Opera, in Cleveland, and in Philadelphia. It was also heard from one end of Europe to another—from

the London radio with Albert Coates conducting, to Bratislava, Czecholovakia. *Lady Macbeth* was conquering the world.

But how could such fame be tolerated in the land of "equality and brotherhood"? Why is Shostakovich being performed everywhere? What's so special about him? The international recognition of that Soviet composer was bound to cost him something in his own country. He had dared to outgrow the scale the Party had been measuring him by. He had to be whittled down to size—reduced to the general level of Soviet culture, to so-called Socialist Realism. The Composer's Union—save for a few outstanding composers like Sergei Prokofiev, Aram Khachaturian, Reinhold Glière, and Nikolai Myaskovsky—was made up of nonentities who packed Party cards and sucked up to the great Stalin and the Party with their worthless odes and marches. Shostakovich's genius and personality were more than out of place in that milieu. Amid that stifling mediocrity and pretense, his brilliance and honesty looked positively indecent.

On January 28, 1936, a month after the premiere of *Lady Macbeth* at the Bolshoi, the composer read about his opera in a crushing, crudely vicious *Pravda* article entitled "A Muddle Instead of Music." (And a few days later, on February 5, it was followed by another acerbic article, "Ballet Fakery," written about *The Sparkling Steam*.)

> From the very first minute of the opera, the listener is dumbfounded by a deliberately dissonant, confused flow of sounds. Fragments of melody, the beginnings of a musical phrase, sink down, break loose, and again vanish in the din, grinding and screeching. To follow this "music" is hard, and to remember it is impossible.
>
> . . . The composer of *Lady Macbeth of Mtsensk* had to borrow his nervous, convulsive, epileptic music from jazz in order to endow his characters with "pas-

> sion" . . . At a time when our criticism—including music criticism—is pledged to Socialist Realism, the stage serves up to us, in the work of Shostakovich, the crudest kind of naturalism.
>
> And all of it is crude, primitive, vulgar . . . The music quacks, moans, pants, and chokes in order to render the love scenes as naturally as possible. And "love" is smeared all over the opera in the most vulgar form.

In the Party's ideological war, Shostakovich was the first musician to take a blow, and he realized it was a fight to the death for his conscience as an artist and creator. In the Soviet Union, the appearance in *Pravda* of an article like that is tantamount to a command: beat him, cut him down, tear him to pieces. The victim is tagged an enemy of the people, and a gang of worthless characters, openly supported by the top Party echelon, rushes forward to curry favor and make their careers. A fall from a big horse is bound to be painful: Shostakovich was badly wounded by that blow from the government, with which he had never had a confrontation before. But he did not accept their "criticism"; he did not repent. For two years he wrote no response, although they fully expected him to. And however Soviet musicologists may try today, as they collect his public statements crumb by crumb, they can't find anything from those years. It was a heroic silence, a symbol of disloyalty and resistance to the regime. And very few would have been able to do as he did. Shostakovich kept quiet and to himself, not speaking his mind until two years later. He finally made his statement on November 21, 1937, in Philharmonic Hall in Leningrad with his Fifth Symphony, that extraordinary masterpiece, which, as our Dmitri Dmitriyevich told us, was autobiographical.

Listening to it, we become aware of the agonies he lived through. In that music, Shostakovich speaks on the events of those years with more passion and courage than any writer or painter who bore witness to those times. The Fifth Symphony was a turning point not only in his creative life but in his outlook as a Russian. He became the chronicler of our country; the history of Soviet Russia is nowhere better described than in his compositions.

No, Shostakovich did not betray his art. He did not repent, he did not pound his chest in public, pledging henceforth to be an ordinary Socialist-Realist mediocrity. But neither did he come out and openly defend his position. He knew that, during those years of terror, he simply would have been asking to be annihilated. He did not have the right to concede his life to the insatiable Moloch without having done another small part of what he could do best and what God had ordered him to do. Through agonizing searching, through struggle and suffering, he found the only way out: the lie. He could lie if it meant the salvation of his own creativity.

Before the Fifth Symphony was allowed to be performed, it was heard by the Party *aktiv* in Leningrad. A few dozen nincompoops got together to judge a genius: to make objections, to lecture him, and in general to teach him how to write music. He had to save his newborn from their talons. But how? He tried to deceive them in the most rudimentary way, and succeeded! All he had to do was use other words to describe the huge complex of human passions and suffering that is so apparent in his music—he described his music to the Party as joyous and optimistic—and the entire pack dashed off, satisfied. The Fifth Symphony, safe from their clutches, resounded throughout the world, announcing the sufferings of great Russia that had been written in the blood of our contemporary. Yes, he had found a way to live and create in that country . . .

But he had learned to put on a mask he would wear for the rest of his life.

In their essentials, the events that Vishnevskaya describes are not all that historically unusual. A brash young genius generates envy and hostility among his less talented colleagues, and so becomes a target of the jealous mediocrities who control cultural life as well as the system of patronage and performance. It's an old story, perhaps most familiar in connection with Mozart and the play/film *Amadeus*. The only twist on what would otherwise resemble a typically cutthroat tale of Social Darwinism in the arts, common to virtually any era, is the political element: the involvement of the Soviet state and the life-and-death consequences of open defiance. Accordingly, much of the controversy surrounding Shostakovich's music to this day revolves around the exact extent to which Vishnevskaya's aptly noted "mask" applies to individual works, and to the composer's various public and private statements about them.

Whatever the reality, it is quite clear that Shostakovich's music meant something very special and quite specific to his contemporaries, whether it be a chronicle of the horrors of Soviet life, as Vishnevskaya so passionately contends, or a more personal message. It's important to stress, however, that all great music has the simultaneous quality of being rooted in the time and circumstances of its composition as well as universal in its broader expressive meaning. This is, in essence, the very definition of what it means to be "classical" in the first place. It's a mistake to assume that because the original circumstances of a work's creation have vanished, it ceases to communicate with a similarly powerful immediacy or relevance to new audiences.

Today's listeners, especially those who are not Russian and did not live through the middle decades of the twentieth century in that country, cannot recapture the desperation, fear, and suffering of the Soviet era other than at second hand. Nevertheless, the emotions expressed by any of Shostakovich's major works, whether joyous or despairing, depend for their depth and truth not on any prior knowledge of the composer or his times but rather on his ability to convey feeling through music. This survey, then, is not based on the notion that the reason for Shostakovich's continued popularity and importance is a function of what his works pretend to say but do not actually mean, or that their true purpose can only be understood by a privileged few who happen to have access to top-secret documents and years of prior study or who shared certain life experiences with the composer himself.

There are instances (the Tenth Symphony being a prime example) where the relationship between the composer's own life and his artistic intentions can be traced with reasonable certainty, or where the audible evidence supports a certain amount of speculation that illuminates a particular work in a musically useful way. I have no intention of letting such opportunities pass by without comment. However, I believe that when all is said and done, the most important factor sustaining Shostakovich's greatness is his music's emotional honesty and expressive clarity, which is in turn of function of its straightforward, no-holds-barred impact in performance.

On this, I think it's safe to say, everyone agrees. The music speaks for itself to those willing to listen attentively. As Vishnevskaya points out, the nature of Shostakovich's game of deception with the authorities was one of verbal misdirection and not musical compromise, since they weren't especially bright or culturally sophisticated and probably disliked most serious compositions anyway. It was a matter of letting them take the easy way out, believing what was said rather than expending the necessary time and effort in forming an independent opinion about what was heard. When you think about it, this approach makes a great deal of practical sense for a composer in Shostakovich's precarious position, revealing a very believable, cynical, and all-too-accurate awareness of the foibles of the party hacks that sat in judgment over him.

Even today, and notwithstanding the uniquely demented policies of the Soviet art-police, it's just as true that a few words, no matter how silly or inapplicable, carry more force with some people that the clear sense of what a piece of music expresses.

Coming from the composer, their effect can be positively deadly, and it doesn't matter what the context or circumstances surrounding their utterance might have been. The desire for a verbal explanation of what a piece of abstract music "means" is so great that virtually any statement will do. Consequently, it's still all too common to read commentaries in program notes at concerts as well as CD booklets consisting almost entirely of biographical trivia and mythology, often to the point where the music itself gets lost in the shuffle. Discussion of a work's supposedly hidden "message" ignores the far more important elements lying right there on the surface, to which the listener's attention should be directed.

There is, in fact, a curious reluctance to speak of these pieces in musical terms that would otherwise seem quite natural in considering the output of other composers. This is particularly odd in Shostakovich's case, since from the very beginning, his individuality and talent were extremely evident, and as you will see and hear, the elements of his style are unusually easy to discern. I'm thinking of matters of form, melodic content, rhythm, orchestration, harmony—all areas in which Shostakovich was a master with very recognizable fingerprints. It's even not unusual to see him criticized as formally or melodically deficient, and his music damned with faint praise as getting by on sheer character and emotional hysteria alone (criticisms also leveled for some time at the composer whom Shostakovich often resembles more than any other: Mahler).

So I propose to make a fresh start: to come to the music without any preconceptions or prejudices, save the proposition that Shostakovich was arguably Russia's greatest symphonic composer, and this fact has less to do with his environment than with his genius as a musical thinker and his ability to create a personal language of universal appeal. The purpose of this book is to define and describe the musical elements of that language to you: what it sounds like and how it works expressively. This is distinct from the practice of analysis, which is more concerned with the mechanics of composition from a technical point of view. Instead, in this "owner's manual," I will introduce the fifteen symphonies and six concertos in turn, chronologically, offering a sort of guided tour to what you will hear as each piece unfolds before you in real time. Quite a few other important and worthwhile Shostakovich works will be mentioned as well, as an aid to additional listening beyond the immediate scope of this book.

Accompanying you on this musical journey is a CD containing a fine performance of Shostakovich's most popular symphony (the Fifth). This will be discussed first. In this way, you can hear most of the various elements that comprise his individual style. Additionally, hearing a piece whole permits discussion of large-scale form and organization, a subject usually ignored or downplayed when considering Shostakovich's music, but an area in which his imagination and creativity are no less marked, and no less successful, than in more obvious compositional skills (such as orchestration). This may be a controversial point for some, since the treatment of form isn't supposedly one of Shostakovich's strengths. Indeed, it is often considered, with some reason, a weakness of the Russian school in general, from Tchaikovsky and Rimsky-Korsakov onwards.

Shostakovich, however, was one of the very few composers who reinvigorated classical symphonic structures by adapting them to his music's particular expressive needs. In so doing, he effectively created new versions of such tried-and-true forms as sonata, passacaglia, toccata, and rondo, among others. This may sound dry and uninteresting, but it really isn't. In fact, it's fascinating and, more to the point, very helpful as an aid to listening. Powerful emotional expression cannot exist without an equally powerful treatment of form, because any large work lasting more than a few minutes will quickly turn boring and dissipate its energy and intensity, absent some clearly articulated means of organization and contrast that listeners can readily grasp. In Shostakovich's most successful symphonies and concertos, form and content are as inseparable and perfectly equalized as in any piece by the great masters of the classical period (Haydn, Mozart, and Beethoven).

The reason this aspect of Shostakovich's art receives so little mention probably stems from the ironic happenstance that his artistic maturity coincides with the period in which he was first attacked by the authorities and created the Fifth Symphony. Consequently, certain elements of his style, particularly the ones that embrace a more traditional approach to form, are sometimes regarded as tainted, the result of an uncomfortable compromise between his musical vision and the need to toe the party line to a greater or lesser extent. Adding fuel to this particular fire is the fact that the great works of Shostakovich's maturity, what might be called his middle period (taking in Symphonies Nos. 5–10), are more harmonically conservative, and therefore more easily digested, than his often highly dissonant and experimental early pieces. Commentators, especially Russian expatriates, are thus left in an uncomfortable position: that of having to explain that the works on which Shostakovich's worldwide esteem largely rests owe some measure of their success to the compromises that they tacitly accept. In other words, the Soviet authorities weren't entirely wrong.

Once again, Vishnevskaya's remarks offer the key to unraveling this conundrum. She puts her finger on the basic difference between Shostakovich's early and mature music: its increasingly overt emotionalism. This was not something that happened overnight, nor was it the result of the scandal of 1936. Both the Fourth Symphony and the opera *Lady Macbeth of Mtsensk* show him clearly headed in this direction. Unfortunately, the opera was later revised and "cleaned up" to make it more palatable (a version long shelved in favor of the original), and the Fourth Symphony was suppressed until the 1960s, making assessment of the composer's development from the cool brilliance of his early works to the supercharged, romantic ethos of his later ones a more complicated subject than it ought to be.

Whether or not the Fifth Symphony would have taken its present form without the abuse and fear of the years immediately preceding its composition is a moot point. Stylistically, it could only have been written by Shostakovich, whatever the mix of ingredients that it employs. Beyond that, the history of twentieth-century music teaches an inviolable rule: composers may write in any style they choose, but if they want their music to express human feelings in such a way that audiences of discerning and serious listeners will understand, then they have to adapt their own style (at least to some degree) to a generally accepted language that adheres to certain tried-and-true conventions. In other words, the music has to be largely tonal and based on the presentation and development of clearly discernable ideas, motives, and tunes. There's no getting around this basic fact, however interesting or valid music conceived along entirely different lines may be.

For whatever reason, from about the early 1930s onwards, Shostakovich decided that this was the kind of composer he wished to become, and as the results prove, he was terrifically good at it. I would argue, then, that to the extent the actual events of 1936 influenced the direction of his creative life, they forced him to confront a series of issues that were as much (and as legitimately) musical as they were ideological, social, or political. All composers, no matter what their circumstances, have to answer the question of what kind of artists they are, what they want their art to express, who their audience is, and what level of acceptance they want their works to enjoy. In this particular case, the works immediately prior to 1936 conclusively reveal

Shostakovich moving towards the Russian musical mainstream, absorbing into his personal idiom certain elements of late nineteenth- and early twentieth-century romanticism, including the heroic tone, epic scale, and characteristic expressive extremes. This is what listeners so clearly heard at the premiere of the Fifth Symphony.

Adopting a romantic aesthetic also presupposes an emphasis on the subjective feelings of the artist, sometimes at the expense of all other considerations, and Shostakovich's best-known work has often been incorrectly described in such terms. In reality, his mature compositions impose a formal discipline on his highly charged emotionalism that is largely foreign to his early pieces. Even the much-reviled Twelfth Symphony is extremely cogent as regards structure and organization, whatever reservations there might be about its content. Shostakovich is hardly alone in moving from a period of youthful experimentation to a maturity that incorporates conservative (perhaps a better term would be *traditional*) aspects of Western musical practice. In the twentieth century alone, major composers as diverse as Bartók, Copland, Stravinsky, and Hindemith effected a very similar accommodation and stylistic evolution, without being accused of selling out (save by those with some sort of ideological axe to grind).

Shostakovich's triumph, as Vishnevskaya notes in connection with the Fifth Symphony, lies in the fact that whatever artistic truce he observed in order to survive in the Soviet system, and whatever may have motivated him, it did not diminish the quality of the music he created as a result. And it's not necessary to insist that everything he did is equally good for this point to remain valid. Furthermore, composers of every period have had to deal with adverse conditions and personal tragedy, all of which had an impact on the formation of their respective idioms, a fact so obvious that I hope I needn't belabor it further. The only thing that matters in the final analysis is whether or not they wrote great music. Shostakovich did. Ultimately his work stands or falls on its own very considerable merits, and understanding what these are comprises the substance of the following chapters.

Listening to Shostakovich

Make no mistake: whatever one believes about what Shostakovich is trying to say, his music does speak a personal and emotionally comprehensive language, one present right from the beginning. It is expressively specific and consistently used throughout his career, in all the genres in which he worked. Naturally, each piece employs a different balance of moods and feelings, and these determine whether the overall impression is one of happiness, sadness, and every gradation in between; but because his style is so unmistakable from one work to the next, it makes sense to begin your musical exploration with the music on the accompanying CD, so as to help define the various elements that comprise Shostakovich's stylistic vocabulary. You will then have all the equipment you need to continue exploring the remaining works at your leisure.

Before beginning, there's one important observation about the nature of Shostakovich's musical language that should prove extremely helpful, and this concerns his attitude towards tunes. It has been said by some of his critics that Shostakovich was not a distinguished melodist in the sense that, say, Tchaikovsky and Prokofiev were: filling their best works with catchy, singable melodies in abundance. This observation is certainly true, as far as it goes. However, as a symphonist, what matters most is not how distinctive a tune is but rather what it expresses and what can be made of it over the course of a movement. The film scores and songs reveal Shostakovich as a very capable tunesmith when he wanted to be, but when it comes to the large-scale instrumental works, he was less interested in writing self-contained, independent themes than in how best to convey the emotional trajectory of each movement as a whole.

In short, Shostakovich's style in his instrumental music consists not so much of tunes that you'll come away humming but rather of families of themes and melodies that capture certain kinds of feeling and expression, whether tragic, sarcastic, innocent, joyous, gentle, or brutal. The following work doesn't contain every single category of melodic archetype that he created, but you will hear many of them, and simply knowing what *kind* of idiom he adopts in his large orchestral works will help you in identifying other recurring elements when you encounter them on your own. There is nothing particularly difficult or complicated about this particular style of composition. Many of the greatest composers wrote similarly, including Haydn, Beethoven, Bruckner, and Mahler, to name but a few. Perhaps the most famous of all was Bach, the emotional meaning of whose "tune families" has fascinated scholars and listeners for centuries.

So Shostakovich's work belongs to a remarkable and highly distinguished lineage, and as a symphonist, he was working squarely within a well-established tradition. What distinguished him from so many of his contemporaries, at least on the evidence of the works themselves, was his awareness of this tradition, of what it meant and how best to use it to achieve his own personal expressive ends. Despite the appealing myth of artistic creation being a process of mystical, spontaneous generation, the truth is that raw talent counts for little absent knowledge, excellent training, superior craftsmanship, and a healthy worth ethic. Shostakovich had them all. His music is invariably well made and dead accurate in expressing exactly what he wishes it to, however much wiggle room he leaves for debate as to his precise intentions.

Symphony No. 5
1937

Orchestration: piccolo, 2 flutes, 2 oboes, E-flat clarinet, 2 clarinets, 2 bassoons, contrabassoon, 4 horns, 3 trumpets, 3 trombones, tuba, timpani, triangle, snare drum, bass drum, cymbals, tam-tam, glockenspiel, xylophone, celesta, 2 harps, piano, strings (violins, violas, cellos, basses)*

Discussions of the Fifth Symphony tend to focus so intensely on whether or not the finale represents a genuinely happy ending, to the exclusion of all other factors, that it's easy to overlook an obvious fact: what a piece of music means is not determined by the last note heard but rather by the entire range of emotions expressed—their duration and intensity. This is exactly what Shostakovich meant when he said: "In the compositional center of that symphony, I placed man with all his sufferings, and the finale resolves the tragically tense passages of the first parts on a joyous, optimist plane." The last clause of this statement may be controversial, but the first clause certainly is not. In other words, the music embodies the wholeness of the human personality, and this is true of every one of Shostakovich's large instrumental works, however different the mix of feelings might be in each case.

---

* All orchestration lists give the total number of instruments required, and not the number of players. In the woodwind section, it is quite common for players to "double" within a family. In other words, the flutes also play piccolo, clarinets also take E-flat or bass clarinet, and the contrabassoon may double on bassoon, as necessary.

There is plenty of emotional variety in this symphony even before the finale bursts in, including triumph, despair, violence, tranquility, innocence, mystery, vulgarity, and humor. Its greatness is a function of the totality. Beyond that, perhaps the most interesting fact about the ending is how logically and organically it arises from what has come before. This is why in describing the work, it's important to get beyond a subjective account of the feelings the music arouses and also give due consideration to questions of formal coherence—how each part fits into Shostakovich's overall scheme of contrasts, and contributes to the variety and balance of emotions that the symphony expresses.

First Movement: Moderato (CD track 1)

Like many of Shostakovich's first movements, this one is in sonata form, but a uniquely personal version of it. By the late romantic period, the sonata idea meant something very different than it had originally when it was perfected in the second half of the eighteenth century by Haydn, assisted later by Mozart and Beethoven. Learning the difference between the various incarnations of this form isn't important for understanding Shostakovich, nor is one type inherently superior to another. What matters is whether or not the forms a composer uses are well suited to what the music says. All you need to know for present purposes is that for Shostakovich, as for most other composers from the late nineteenth century onwards, a sonata-form movement has three sections: an *exposition* that presents the main thematic material, a *development* that manipulates this material in various theoretically exciting and moving ways, and a *recapitulation/coda* that restates the music of the exposition, often in considerably altered form, by way of ultimately arriving at a satisfying conclusion.

Symphony No. 5

Exposition

Many of Shostakovich's major works, including Symphonies Nos. 6, 8, 10, and 14, as well as both violin concertos and the Second Cello Concerto, begin with a slow, sad elegy primarily for strings. The music that opens this symphony constitutes the first of them. Cellos and basses, answered by the violins, lead off in close *canon* (meaning that one part overlaps the other, playing the same music at a fixed distance). And like most of the examples just listed, the shape of this initial threnody is circular—that is, the opening gesture returns after various contrasting ideas or short episodes. Using letters to represent each section, the entire opening paragraph (or *first subject*) of the Fifth Symphony has the shape ABACADA, with every recurrence of A subtly varied. Here is a brief description of each section:

A: Pay particular attention to the first two rising notes, the jagged rhythm, and the dying fall with which this opening motive concludes, consisting of a chain of three-note figures.

B (at 0:28): This is the real principal theme of the first subject, a descending phrase on violins over a string accompaniment consisting of A's first two notes. The melody also contains more of the three-note figures.

A (at 1:02): A creepy transformation on bassoons and *pizzicato* (plucked) cellos and basses.

C (at 1:28): The first violins continue their melody freely, the omnipresent three-note figures marking this idea out as a continuation of B. Flutes join in at the tune's high points, and the oboe phrase at 2:37 is going to become quite important as the symphony progresses.

A (at 2:49): Violins have the tune over a rolling accompaniment in cellos and bassoon, while horns take over the dying cadence.

D (at 3:15): Horns, joined by violins, return to the continually evolving B melody and pass it off to the trumpets in a brilliant but dissonant climax. Remember these stabbing repeated notes. They represent one of the main motives of the entire symphony and show up in many guises.

A (at 3:43): In canon once again between violins, and violas plus cellos, the opening motive appears one last time, answered yet again by the horns.

An important aside: notice the lack of low brass and percussion. Shostakovich has a reputation for being a very heavy, dark-sounding, and seriously loud composer, but his scoring is extremely transparent and never has any padding, and he's always willing to keep something in reserve for a more effective entrance later on. So far, in the first several minutes of the symphony, he has used only two flutes, two oboes, three clarinets, two bassoons, four horns, two trumpets, and strings. Nothing more.

Most sonata expositions have two main subjects, but keep in mind that there's no limit to how many themes, motives, or ideas comprise a subject. These subjects are separated from each other in most cases by changes of key, texture, rhythm, and volume. For all its abundance of material, there is no question that the entire musical complex just described constitutes a single idea. The second subject turns out to be even more sparsely scored than the first, although it introduces the harps, piccolo, and contrabassoon, all used with great restraint. It too has its own internal shape, EFE:

E (at 4:01): Over a gently pulsing string rhythm and the soft, unbroken chords typical of Shostakovich's writing for the harp, the violins sing out a coolly beautiful melody that turns out to be nothing less than the opening motive (A) in long notes, with the rhythm evened out. So not only is this movement in sonata form, it is in what's called *monothematic*

Symphony No. 5

sonata form, meaning all its important ideas derive from its first subject group. Famous earlier examples include Haydn's Symphony No. 88 and Beethoven's Seventh Symphony.

F (at 5:00): This section contains a whole series of motives, the most important of which is a different take on those three-note figures from the opening theme. Indeed, at 6:15 the music seems to want to head back to the first subject's B or C sections, but instead the previous theme returns (E), this time a bit darker, on the violas, dissolving into more three-note motives, now distinctly ominous.

Development (at 7:27)

The tempo picks up as the development section begins with the piano hammering out three-note figures in its lowest register. It's a wonderfully threatening sound, as is the snarling entry of the horns and trumpets with the main theme of the first subject (B). Shostakovich often increases the speed of his developments, highlighting the fact that although the word *development* sounds technical, it's actually the part of the movement where the most dramatic events take place. Pay particular attention to the new theme that the woodwinds generate out of previously heard material at 8:05. It's an amalgam of B plus an extended version of the oboe melody at 2:37 in the exposition (section C). This idea will return to conclude the movement and also feature in both the scherzo and finale.

To a galloping rhythm on the trumpets similar to that in Rossini's *William Tell* overture (another ubiquitous Shostakovich fingerprint), the music rushes swiftly to its first climax, including the initial appearance of the trombones and tuba. With a crash on the cymbals, the trumpets, snare drum, and timpani turn the first subject's B theme into a grotesque, goose-stepping march. This technique of brutalizing a formerly lyrical melody is something that Shostakovich learned from Mahler. The xylophone eventually takes over the Rossini rhythm, tapping it out on one note, before the march briefly returns and the music collapses into the depths.

Now comes the movement's big climax (at 10:14). Violins frantically scream out the opening motive in canon with the lower strings, while on top, the brass play another canon consisting of the second-subject long-note version of the same tune. So as you can plainly hear, this terrifying and dramatic passage results from the strict logic of the movement's thematic design and ongoing development. The form serves the expressive content, as with all great pieces of music. As the strings and brass carry their contest onward and upward, the tempo begins to slow down by degrees. One of the acid tests for conductors of this symphony is how well they time and control this particular ritard. With another crash on the cymbals (at 10:51), the music spills over into the:

Recapitulation

The idea of making the moment of recapitulation the climax of the development section is not new. You can hear it, for example, in the opening movements of Brahms's First Symphony and Tchaikovsky's Fourth, to name just two famous instances. But Shostakovich not only adopted this process more extensively than just about any other composer, he often prolongs the climax by recomposing the first subject as a massive orchestral cataclysm. This is what happens here, as well as in Symphonies Nos. 7, 8, 10, and 13. In the less tragic first movements of works such as Symphonies Nos. 1, 9, and 12, as well as in most of the concertos, he still often preserves the idea of a musical climax timed to coincide with the arrival of the recapitulation, but the degree of violence tends to be less, depending on the character of the individual themes.

Here, the entire first subject gets compressed into a grand unison for full orchestra, interrupted by exclamations from the brass, cymbals, and timpani. The music peaks on the oboe phrase from the first subject (the one at 2:37), and with a crash on the tam-tam, trombones and tuba blast out the symphony's opening idea in an angry diminuendo. Again notice the stabbing, single-note rhythmic accompaniment, which slowly fades away on trumpets and pounding timpani. A pastoral major-key reprise of the second subject now takes shape as a duet between flute and horn (at 12:00), with two taps on the glockenspiel adding a touch of color. Many composers have a particular fondness for specific instruments, and this passage highlights the two that always seem to get "most favored" treatment in Shostakovich's orchestral works. This horn solo is treacherous, being both very high and very soft.

Like the first subject, the second is extremely foreshortened, getting as far as an abbreviated version of its middle section (F) before sinking back into darkness. Strings begin the nocturnal minor-key coda (at 13:49) with the same accompaniment—based on the opening theme—that they had at the beginning of the symphony. Over this dark texture, flute, piccolo, and solo violin take turns with that oboe phrase from the first subject, while the strings pulse delicately below and the harp adds flecks of color. In answer to the distant summons of the trumpets and timpani, the celesta brings the movement to an unforgettable pianissimo close with three rising scales.

Second Movement: Allegretto (CD track 2)

Most scherzos, based as they are on the idea of a comparatively simple dance movement, have a basic ABA structure, and this one is no exception—although Shostakovich also uses ABAB (in the Sixth and Fifteenth Symphonies, for example) and even full sonata form (in the Eighth). Cellos and basses lead off as at the beginning of the symphony, but what they play is in fact a variant of the first subject's main melody (B), which by now you have heard lots of times and so may well notice the similarity. It's also worth pointing out that all the tunes in the outer sections of this movement feature those stabbing repeated-note figures as well.

After the opening melody for cellos and basses, mocking woodwinds squeal in with yet another variation, this time a witty parody, of the entire B section (at 0:17). Just compare what sounds like the arrival of a new, dancelike idea at 0:55 to what the violins play in the first movement at 8:28. Thematic transformations like this are very common in Shostakovich, and their point is not to suggest some hidden meaning or subtext but rather to give the entire work a feeling of organic unity: to suggest, even subconsciously, that all its various parts somehow belong together.

This particular idea is also a very close relative to the main theme of the finale of the First Cello Concerto. It alternates with a brazen march on horns, timpani, and snare drum, with some spicy repeated-note commentary from the violins, ultimately leading to the central episode, or *trio* section in musical jargon, at 1:48. This has two parts, both of which get repeated: A (solo violin with harp), A (solo flute with harp), B (strings lead, at 2:32), B (woodwinds lead). The opening section returns, recast for pizzicato strings and witty bassoon, and leads to a mostly regular repeat of the initial material. Like the scherzo of Beethoven's Ninth Symphony, this one makes as if it wants to return to the trio section yet again, but the rest of the orchestra dismisses that notion and finishes rudely, with clattering xylophone to the fore.

Third Movement: Largo (CD track 3)

Perhaps the most important fact about this movement—and the key to the haunting, otherworldly quality of its emotional intensity—is that no brass instruments participate at all. Shostakovich divides the violin section in three throughout and asks for the full compliment of winds, with two harps, piano, xylophone, glockenspiel, and celesta. The result has a misty, luminous quality, touched on at the end of the Fourth Symphony but which will figure ever more prominently in his music as time goes on, particularly in such late works as Symphony No. 11 (first movement), No. 13 (last movement), No. 14 (third song, "Loreley"), and No. 15 (second movement). The main theme is a lyrical expansion of the mood—not the melody—of the first movement's second subject, and you may note a slender thematic connection as well in the largo's opening four notes.

Like the first movement, this one is in sonata form. Because the music moves so slowly—with each repetition of previous material varied in length, scoring, and volume—the usual sectional divisions can be difficult to hear at first. So Shostakovich offers his listeners two very clearly differentiated subjects, thus creating effective contrasts of mood and texture even at these comparatively subdued dynamic levels:

Exposition

First Subject: This beautiful hymn for strings has two halves: the long opening melody, and a sad new idea for violins (at 1:58), whose first two phrases each begin with four repeated notes.
Second Subject (at 2:40): a desolate flute solo (see how important this instrument is for Shostakovich?) with harp accompani-

ment, possibly based on the principal descending violin theme from the first movement.

Development (at 3:26)

This development section, even were it the only bit of Shostakovich's music to survive, would suffice to prove him a musical genius. It has everything: memorable melody and a huge range of emotion, and it is a genuine development, a systematic exploration of the potential of the preceding ideas, along with an important new one. It begins with a return to the first half of the first subject, which slowly reaches a passionate climax over a timpani roll. This passage includes the full complement of strings and woodwind for the first time in the movement. Next, wispy string tremolos introduce a lonely pastoral theme for solo oboe (at 5:14). This alternates with bits of the hymnlike opening theme. Notice how, at 6:17, when the clarinet gets this new idea, Shostakovich combines it with the first subject's second half (the melody that began with four repeated notes at 1:58).

A last repetition of the pastoral theme, this time on flute, leads to a new variant of the entire first subject, initially on low woodwinds but quickly rising to the movement's main climax on reaching the melody's second half—its four-repeated-note figure hammered out by violins and xylophone over intense tremolos on strings and piano. This rises upwards in an anguished, screaming crescendo; cuts off; and then cellos surge forward with a desperate, urgent version of the previous section's pastoral woodwind melody, later combined with the first subject on the violins (at 10:09). The scoring here is marvelous: just strings and clarinets at first, yet you may well remember it as the most powerful moment in the symphony. It's a particularly vivid example of how restraint can become a musical force in its own right.

The climax finally grinds to a halt, and Shostakovich offers a highly abbreviated recapitulation: first subject on ghostly muted strings, with the second—which was entirely absent from the development section—given to high violins and harps. This slowly spirals back down to earth on the cellos and basses, and over a high violin tremolo, harps and celesta tap out a coda. It's the woodwind tune from the development section, now the very embodiment of ethereal stillness. Two soft chords from the remaining strings bring the movement to its tranquil close, a stunning marriage of pure symphonic form and profoundly moving emotional content.

Finale: Allegro non troppo (CD track 4)

Understanding the possible meanings of this finale requires that a couple of points be emphasized up front. First, whether or not you accept its purported triumph at face value, the movement is still, above all, a satisfying culmination of the symphony on purely musical grounds. Second, not all symphonies conclude with their longest, most expressive, and therefore most important movement. In fact, the majority do not. This is one of the things that Shostakovich might have meant when in his purported and controversial memoir, *Testimony,* he asked rhetorically, "What exultation can there be?" especially after the intensity of feeling expressed in the largo. This strikes me as a very fair question. Taken on its own, the finale is not as long or complex as the first movement, nor as lyrical or spiritually involving as the largo. That doesn't mean it's not a good piece or the right finale for this particular work, but it does suggest where the heart of the symphony truly lies.

There are in fact three possible views of this concluding movement from which listeners may choose: that the victory at the end is real, that it is false, or that while offering a musically effective conclusion to the symphony, the ending does not alter its overall emotional character. At one time or another, I have subscribed to all three of these notions. It depends on the interpretation, one's own mood, and a host of other contingent factors. And that's the beauty of great music: it presents different facets on different occasions, and it isn't necessary to favor one view over another, as long as they all remain consistent with the musical facts.

This piece is also in sonata form, but a different variety than either the first movement or the largo. There are two well-defined subjects, so it is not monothematic, but the recapitulation and coda are combined and omit the second subject entirely. In short, the form is truncated, a clear sign that Shostakovich does not intend that the finale operate with the same degree of expressive depth and sophistication as those other two movements. Indeed, the exciting opening theme, for brass over pounding timpani, is designed to shatter the mood of the largo's closing pages as crudely as possible. Compare this passage to the similar tactic used by Mahler to contrast the third and fourth movements of his First Symphony, or fourth and fifth movements of his Second.

Like its counterpart in the opening movement, this first subject has a "verse and refrain" shape, with the brass theme returning in between energetic contrasting material for strings and woodwinds. Much of this is based, however freely, on previously heard material. The finale's pounding timpani mirror the initial first-movement string accompaniment to the principal theme, and the important oboe phrase that ultimately brought that movement to a close (and also featured in the scherzo) appears here at 0:33 and 0:55. The second subject is a lyrical trumpet solo surrounded by a maelstrom of swirling strings and woodwinds (at 2:31). It seems headed for a collapse, backed by an insistently tapping xylophone, but instead makes one more sweeping effort on the violins, only to be obliterated by a cymbal crescendo and crash on the tam-tam. The frantically pounding timpani and furious low brass writing strikingly recall the climax of the first movement, which is again part of the point: this music has no independent existence of its own. It is a summary of what has come before, and not a new dawn.

The development section (at 3:42) begins as a nostalgic horn solo with a sad remembrance of the second subject. Violins take over in a tearful lament that recalls the music from the largo, while the woodwinds answer (at 4:51) with a transformation of the first movement's oboe motive. Next, atop a wavering figure in the violins, bits of the first subject come and go (at 5:14). Cellos and basses take over this accompaniment, leaving the violins free to spin out a sad, somewhat mysterious melody that reaches all the way back to the coda of the first movement for a similar atmosphere. As the accompaniment resurfaces, the harps pick it up (at 6:56) in a clear, hopeful recollection of the largo's second subject. In just a few short minutes, all at very low volume, Shostakovich has summarized much of the content of the entire symphony, reminding everyone where the music has been and what it has endured.

The positive ending of the development section is immediately negated by quiet riffs on the snare drum, and beating timpani. Slowly, the first subject gathers itself in clarinets and bassoons. Notice the increasing prevalence of repeated-note figures—first in the woodwinds, then in the violins as they enter (at 8:25) after a long pause. These stabbing single-note motives have been poking at the music, and at the brains of its listeners, since the first movement. Now they begin to take over the texture entirely. The trumpets rise up with the opening of the first subject, and with a crash of the cymbals, the music explodes into a triumphant major key. Crunching chords from the brass and bass drum (saved for this entrance) signal defiance. The horns take over, joined by the trumpets, while the violins spiral higher and higher with their repeated-note figures.

Trumpets, clashing dissonantly with the violins, peal out over a big ritard, until a snare-drum crescendo, leading to a huge crash on cymbals and bass drum, clears the air. Violins and piano hammer away repeatedly at a single note, while the brass, capped by cymbals and triangle, reiterate bits of the first subject over pounding timpani. This smashing and bashing, with the strings pinging away on top, continues with ever-increasing relentlessness, then cuts off abruptly, leaving timpani and bass drum to drive home the final unison. Ironically, such a thunderous peroration is actually atypical for Shostakovich: only the Seventh and Twelfth Symphonies do something similar. Nevertheless, it has become the stereotypical example of what his music is supposed to sound like.

Beyond the question of its ending, the Fifth Symphony bears out Vishnevskaya's contention that the real victory here was Shostakovich's. The work is deliberately traditional in form, but the almost insolent compositional virtuosity with which Shostakovich deploys his three very different examples of the sonata style certainly throws down the gauntlet to those who felt that by forcing him to write in a more conservative idiom, they would cripple his talent and mute his expressive intensity (or channel it differently). In fact, they achieved just the opposite. The genie was out of the bottle for good.

Part 2

Early-Period Works

Symphony No. 1
1924–25

Orchestration: piccolo, 3 flutes, 2 oboes, 2 clarinets (B-flat and A), 2 bassoons, 3 trumpets, 4 horns, 3 trombones, tuba, timpani, triangle, snare drum, bass drum, cymbals, tam-tam, glockenspiel, piano, strings

The First Symphony is an amazing piece for a nineteen-year old to have written. Intended as a graduation exercise from Leningrad Conservatory, the music features many of the formal and stylistic characteristics that Shostakovich would continue to mine fruitfully for the remainder of his career. It's also a timely reminder, in the face of all the controversy regarding his life, of just what a startling musical genius he was. The great classical prodigies (Mozart, Schubert, Mendelssohn) also created their first masterpieces at about age eighteen, however much of their precocious youthful stuff additionally survives. Shostakovich was without a doubt in that league, and this symphony certainly stands among the most mature and consistently successful efforts by a youthful composer, irrespective of historical period.

The examiners at the conservatory, headed by Alexander Glazunov, declared that Shostakovich possessed "a distinctive and striking creative talent." So much so, in fact, that this remains the only Russian symphony in the active international repertoire written between Prokofiev's "Classical" Symphony (1918) and Shostakovich's own Fourth (1935–36) and Fifth (1937). Like the Prokofiev, this too is very much a "classical" symphony, both formally and expressively: a witty, brilliant work, but one that in its slow movement strikes a deeper emotional note than does that of Shostakovich's elder colleague. It's no surprise that the First Symphony became an instant international success, and it continues to offer striking evidence of a dazzling young talent displaying his natural gifts as a symphonist while in full command of his personal idiom.

First Movement: Allegretto

If you followed the previous discussions of the Fifth Symphony and Second Cello Concerto, you will find yourself on familiar formal ground here. This movement employs Shostakovich's patented brand of sonata form, here at a moderate tempo and in a particularly clear way. Indeed, the cut of this movement is so deliberately schematic and obvious that it becomes a source of humor all by itself and serves to emphasize the music's brittle neoclassicism. All of Shostakovich's best music has a certain twitchy, nervous edge, even when it's trying to ingratiate itself to the listener (not as unusual an occurrence as some would have you believe), and this quality was present right from the start. It's a function of pungent harmony, jerky rhythms, a fondness for the woodwind family (piccolo, flute, and bassoon especially), and a melodic line that gets tossed in bits from one orchestral section to the next.

In keeping with the basics of sonata form, the exposition has two subjects, and the first of these, typically for Shostakovich, is one of his mini-rondo shapes: ABACADA. Muted trumpet, lachrymose bassoon, and strident clarinet lead off, tossing bits of sour melody between them. The orchestral textures are thin, chamberlike, and completely unblended, with each instrument

Symphony No. 1

behaving like a soloist. Listen for the entry of the double basses: this signals B. It leads rapidly back to A, this time on the violins, accelerating into C: a series of repeated-note phrases for violins, then trumpets, interspersed with woodwind squeals. One last pass through A, again on the violins, and an extended march (D) takes shape on solo clarinet, gaining energy and heavier orchestration as it progresses. A climactic cymbal crash initiates a return to the opening phrase on solo trumpet, but pizzicato strings suddenly interrupt with an entirely new rhythm.

While just as lightly scored as its predecessor, the second subject is otherwise as highly contrasted as can be. It's a waltz, a triple-time dance as opposed to the preceding duple-meter march, featuring solo flute accompanied by the most delicate gestures from the strings. Where the first subject was all sardonic fits and starts, this lilting melody expresses purity and innocence in long-breathed phrases. The music's balletic quality recalls the kind of thing Stravinsky was doing at the same time; or perhaps it represents Shostakovich's tribute to Glazunov, a famous ballet composer (*The Seasons, Raymonda*) and head of the Leningrad Conservatory. Shostakovich reputedly disliked Glazunov's somewhat conventional brand of Russian romanticism while respecting the man, and this flute melody perfectly expresses that ambivalence. Is it just too well behaved to be true? Almost before you can make up your mind, the tune comes to a full stop.

The development section is extremely short and based mostly on idea A from the first subject, with just a hint of the second subject's waltz along the way. It rises swiftly to a big climax that, also in keeping with Shostakovich's later practice, initiates the recapitulation. This consists of the march (D) blasted out by the full orchestra in all its militant glory, with gleeful percussion and triumphant horns. Shostakovich's discipline and restraint are remarkable here: consider how long he has waited before unleashing the full power of the orchestra for the very first time.

Because the development spent so much time working with the first subject, its reappearance now is severely abbreviated, making the return of the waltz—again on solo flute—even more abrupt than previously. Its minimal previous contribution permits Shostakovich to give it the full treatment in the recapitulation, and this time around, it leads to an extensive coda that begins with another march-climax on D, which disintegrates into the same fragmented textures and motives with which the symphony began. Woodwinds and triangle wave goodbye with a sly wink, but soft strings have the final word. Altogether, this movement reveals a thoroughly classical poise and wit. Shostakovich does not merely use traditional forms like a good student: he understands what they mean and bends them to his own expressive purposes.

Second Movement: Allegro

The form of this scherzo is simple: ABAB, but it has several delightful subtleties that greatly enhance its character and vividness. First of all, the A sections are not in the usual triple time but in duple meter, like one of Shostakovich's numerous ballet gallops. The opening is very amusing, with cellos and basses seemingly out of sync and a clarinet that can't remember how the tune should go, until a dashing run down the keyboard from the piano sets the violins on the right track. At the time that he was composing this symphony, Shostakovich was making a living playing piano in the theatre, accompanying silent films. It's difficult not to believe that some of his experience has rubbed off here. The movement has a music-hall or operetta-like quality to it that will come to characterize many of Shostakovich's scherzos.

As happened in the first movement, this initial idea stops suddenly, interrupted by a new theme in slow triple time, although the waltz character isn't at all pronounced. The music strongly resembles the Berceuse (Lullaby) from Stravinsky's *The Firebird* and has an exotic, quasi-oriental character. It's one of the few moments in the symphony that might be considered uncharacteristic of Shostakovich's future development, although the scoring, with prominent bassoons, is certainly typical. This B section leads gradually back to the beginning, solo piano well to the fore as previously. The music rises swiftly to a climax in which both sections' principal tunes are combined in exciting counterpoint until a sudden pause, broken only by crashing chords on the piano, introduces the furtive coda. With seemingly wry indifference, the movement tiptoes to a quiet close.

Third Movement: Lento

The slow movement has the same basic shape as the scherzo: ABAB, even down to a contrapuntal combination of its two main themes when the second section comes back towards the end. Technically this formal shape is a kind of sonata form, only without a development section. Mozart was particularly fond of this structure and used it very frequently in his mature music. As you can hear, Shostakovich liked it as well, so much so that he based an entire symphony (the Sixth) on it.

All the contrasts in this symphony are abrupt, but that between the end of the second movement and the beginning of the third may be the most startling of all. In the first place, this lento seems to start with a tune already in progress. There's no introduction or prelude: just an oboe singing a lament on a soft cushion of strings. Second, after two movements characterized by their nervous, disjointed, emotionally brittle qualities, this romantic outpouring of heartfelt sadness comes as a shock. As the melody gains intensity, trumpets and trombones, backed by the snare drum, cut through the texture with a threatening, militant rhythmic motive. This doom-laden atmosphere will become one of the most potent weapons in Shostakovich's expressive arsenal, although in later works, it appears in places other than just the slow movement.

The second subject, in a slightly slower tempo, also features solo oboe and has the character of a funeral march. Note that Shostakovich inserts the threatening rhythmic motive (on the trumpets) here as well. This section rises to a sonorous climax featuring the full brass section, before the lower strings and a brief clarinet solo initiate the recapitulation, with the initial oboe theme now sung passionately by the violins. More rhythmic eruptions from the brass and snare drum accompany a last reminder of the funeral march on muted trumpet, combined with a bit of the main theme in the cellos and basses. The music creeps delicately to a close as luminous solo strings repeat the rhythmic motive (dum, dadadummm, dum, dum) over and over, growing progressively softer and purged of all anxiety. Just as the music seems ready to fade out entirely, a rolling snare drum sneaks in with a crescendo, leading without pause to the:

Fourth Movement: Finale (Lento–Allegro molto)

Actually, some performances omit the snare-drum link between the two movements, supposedly a reflection of Shostakovich's later thoughts—a bit of oral tradition not at all uncommon in the world of classical music, where what performers do isn't always reflected in what gets published. But the drum roll is still in the score, and it's what you will hear the vast majority of the time. Like the preceding two movements, this finale is in sonata form without development: ABAB, but a very much more sophisticated version of it, since it includes important references back to the previous lento (one argument in favor of ensuring that the two remain attached in the listener's mind).

The movement begins with an upward thrust from cellos and basses, topped by tam-tam and suspended cymbals. Oboes and flutes, then a single oboe and clarinet, continue the mood and tempo of the preceding movement in a melancholy introduction. A minute or two of gloom, and the movement takes off with more of Shostakovich's skittish, burlesque music, sort of a combination of the scherzo's attitude with the first movement's harmonic spice. At the climax of the chaos, violins scream out a symmetrical melody that quickly puts a damper on the festivities, becoming the second subject on solo violin at a slower pace. Flute trills, gentle runs on the glockenspiel, and solo horn all contribute to the atmosphere of fragile calm. After a brief return to the movement's introduction, the first subject returns, once again rising to a huge climax capped by massive trills in strings, woodwinds, and brass.

A sudden crash, a pause, and solo timpani bang out the threatening rhythmic motive from the slow movement (*inverted*—that is, the tune now rises instead of falling). After three repetitions on kettledrums, a solo cello enters with the second subject, accompanied throughout by the rhythmic motive on various instruments. This ignites the finale's lyrical climax, a wonderful moment in which the actual main theme of the lento returns passionately in the violins, leading seamlessly into the finale's own second subject in a quicker tempo. The rest of the movement is coda: a fast windup in which brass and percussion bring the work to a powerful close with a whirlwind of energy and excitement.

The emotional tone of this ending is ambiguous. Although it's loud and emphatic, it would be difficult to call it conventionally happy, particularly given the persistence of minor-key tonal coloring right through the final bars. This is important because much discussion of Shostakovich's work focuses on the meaning of his finales, and so it's worth mentioning that right from the start he was not interested in following the usual "darkness to light, tragedy to triumph" emotional progression so typical of his romantic predecessors. But his finales just as rarely fail to deliver the musical goods.

Symphony No. 2 ("To October")
1927

Orchestration: piccolo, 2 flutes, 2 oboes, 2 clarinets, 2 bassoons, 3 trumpets, 4 horns, 3 trombones, tuba, timpani, triangle, snare drum, bass drum, cymbals, siren, glockenspiel, strings, mixed chorus

The Second Symphony exists in the form that it does because for a brief moment in the late 20s and early 30s, the goals of the 1917 Revolution (modernization, the celebration of industrial life, Communist internationalism) seemed to be compatible with the post–World War I musical avant-garde. Both this work and the Third Symphony bear striking resemblances to the contemporaneous works of composers such as Paul Hindemith (Concerto for Orchestra, *Philharmonisches Konzert*), Sergei Prokofiev (Second Symphony, *The Steel Step*), and Kurt Weill (Symphony No. 1), partaking of a very similar "new objectivity" in which emotional expression is subordinated to a more hard-edged, aggressively impersonal aesthetic. In short, Shostakovich's Second and Third are very much of their time and place.

For this reason, they aren't at all popular, are almost never played live, and probably would never be recorded were it not for the existence of complete symphonic cycles. Add in the atrocious "revolutionary" texts of the concluding choruses of both symphonies, and it's no surprise that even the most die-hard fans of the composer find them hard to love. Shostakovich himself regarded them as "youthful experiments," and while they haven't aged terribly well, they were briefly successful in their day. Certainly they lack nothing in sheer technique (the Second Symphony won first prize from the Leningrad Philharmonic Society); the problem is that they reveal little beyond that. Ultimately, all the aforementioned composers abandoned this idiom after a few years, choosing instead something with a little more expressive meat on its bones, and history has not been kind to those that did not or could not.

The Second Symphony remains Shostakovich's most dissonant, unmelodic major work, an achievement of sorts, and he deserves credit for understanding that, given these facts, it pays to keep it short. Playing for about twenty minutes (or less) in a single movement, this is also his most compact symphony, and despite the lack of consonant harmony, it's really not all that hard to listen to. "Interesting" probably describes it best. Shostakovich was simply too good a composer, with too much curiosity about the potential of the modern symphony orchestra, to write ineffectively or dully, even if there are some impractical moments here and there. For example, the part for factory siren—just a couple of blasts during the final chorus and a very chic touch for Russian music in the 1920s—has seldom if ever been heard (evidently, it's hard to find one that plays a good, clean F-sharp), and most performances avail themselves of the option to substitute normal instruments instead.

Formally the piece is quite simple: it consists of an introduction followed by two chaotic climaxes, leading to the uplifting closing chorus that brings order out of the preceding tumult. The symphony opens with a soft bass-drum roll underpinning a veil of darkness produced by muted strings, much divided, playing various *chromatic* scales (that is, moving in half-steps). The result is quite atonal but soft textured. A muted trumpet sings mournfully above this fog of strings, yielding to a solo tuba, which initiates a march in quicker tempo beginning on cellos and basses. This rises rapidly to a frantic climax on high strings, woodwinds, and trumpets, largely in triplet rhythm (three beats squeezed into the space of two), ending with a brilliant, consonant major-key chord capped by a cymbal crash. With that, the first section of the symphony comes to an end.

Marching cellos and basses, then solo tuba, once again lead off the second episode. Beginning frantically, it settles down quickly to a bizarre trio for solo violin, clarinet, and bassoon playing independent, atonal musical lines. The rest of the woodwind section soon comes screeching in, followed by the rest of the orchestra, in what starts to sound like a loud, full-orchestra version of the chromatic darkness with which the symphony began. This is precisely what the section represents, despite the attempts of the horns to impose an actual melody on the confusion. This section too culminates in a bold climax capped by a cymbal crash, whereupon a sadly expressive viola melody—followed by solo clarinet, then solo violin—leads to a blast from the siren (or the brass), introducing the final chorus.

As noted previously, the words aren't going to win any awards: "We walked, and begged for work and bread; Our hearts were gripped by despair; Factory smokestacks rose into the sky like powerless, clenched fists; Our fear bore the names of Silence, Suffering, and Oppression." So it goes, until the October Revolution occurs to liberate humanity to labor happily in the fields of the collective farms and celebrate the hum of industrial machines. Shostakovich disparaged the text as much as anyone. Still, it's not reasonable to expect anything better from a work written to commemorate the tenth anniversary of the revolution, and he is actually rather kind to the chorus. The parts are singable, and the harmonic style is simpler and more consonant but never banal in the worst Socialist Realist manner that came later.

Even more interestingly, just before the end, the chorus engages in a sort of battle with the forces of darkness from the opening of the symphony, with the last words ("Here are the banners, here are the names of the living generations: October, the Commune, Lenin!") shouted and not sung. So the ending, although loud, is not entirely a sunny, heroic triumph, but rather evocative of struggle and suffering. The text actually supports Shostakovich in this respect, and it has to be conceded that he really does a pretty good job with it, all things considered. Remember, there's no evidence that he approached his task in anything but the most serious way, nor was Shostakovich avowedly apolitical in the way that Hindemith tried to be in the face of the Nazi takeover of Germany.

In the 1920s, the Russian Revolution held out the genuine promise of social and cultural renewal, and this aggressive symphony (as well as the Third) is full of that vigorous fighting spirit. If subsequent events turned hope to terror and disillusionment, with dramatic consequences for Shostakovich's art, they should not blind us to the fact that from the beginning, he was a composer whose free creative spirit was always tempered by a social conscience. While never particularly alluring in a conventional sense, his Second Symphony reveals this quality quite clearly when heard in the context of his work as a whole.

Symphony No. 3 ("The First of May")
1929

Orchestration: piccolo, 2 flutes, 2 oboes, 2 clarinets, 2 bassoons, 3 trumpets, 4 horns, 3 trombones, tuba, timpani, triangle, snare drum, bass drum, cymbals, tam-tam, xylophone, glockenspiel, strings, mixed chorus

Symphonies Nos. 2 and 3 are usually lumped together as Shostakovich's two least popular, but although there are similarities (see the previous chapter for details), the differences are even more pronounced. The Third is much simpler in harmonic style, for example, and isn't afraid to use recognizable melodies more or less throughout. It's at least 50 percent longer than the Second, playing for about half an hour, and it has a much less clear-cut structure. Indeed, Shostakovich declared that his intention was to write a work that had no repetition of melodies, which he largely did—at least from one section to the next. It will help you understand the Third Symphony if you permit me a moment to investigate this outwardly puzzling statement a bit further.

Shostakovich had been quite busy in the two years between this work and its predecessor. Specifically, he had completed two very major pieces: the satirical opera *The Nose*, after Gogol, and the score to the silent film *The New Babylon,* which describes bourgeois decadence at the time of the Paris Commune (1871).

This experience with theatrical music had a strong impact on the Third Symphony. In particular, Shostakovich became interested in the application of film-music techniques to large, abstract works. Indeed, *The New Babylon* is a remarkably cogent, self-contained score all by itself and, at over eighty minutes, Shostakovich's lengthiest orchestral piece of any kind. Now that his film music is being taken seriously, it's possible to recognize this work as probably the major effort of this early period.

The Third Symphony, then, proceeds in a sequence of connected but not necessarily related scenes, the main problem being that absent any clear structure, and despite the well-judged variety and placement of necessary contrasts, the listener has no way to tell where the music is going and why. Interestingly enough, most of Shostakovich's film scores see him writing in closed forms—that is, he does not score moment by moment but rather characterizes whole scenes by imposing some independent shape on the music. In his most cinematic later symphony, the Eleventh, he takes full advantage of not just a careful formal design but also an entire panoply of recurring themes that pop up from one movement to the next.

Here, then, Shostakovich indulges in a never-to-be-repeated experiment, but one that offers comparatively easy music. There are basically two ways to approach it. First, you can simply take it as it comes and imagine it as visually descriptive music in search of its film. Second, you can also look at the symphony as a sort of modern gloss on the finale of Beethoven's Ninth, minus the first three movements. The May Day theme of this symphony, proclaiming the unity and brotherhood of all workers, points up the similarity to Beethoven's setting of Schiller's *Ode to Joy*. It is less contentious than the revolutionary subject of the Second Symphony, and this in turn explains the music's optimistic general tone and more euphonious disposition. Here's how the succession of musical scenes takes shape:

Symphony No. 3

Scene 1 (Allegretto): A pastoral dialogue between two clarinets over a plodding pizzicato accompaniment from cellos and basses.

Scene 2 (Più mosso [faster]): The tempo increases as pizzicato strings set up a steady march rhythm, while the trumpet enters with a jaunty new theme. Suddenly the music speeds up yet again, and for the next few minutes, march fragments, mainly on the brass and woodwinds, rapidly alternate with frenetic outbursts in freer rhythm. Note the frequently unblended colors: strings, then winds, then brass, in alternation. It all culminates in a series of noisy collisions between the trumpets and everyone else, capped by cymbal crashes and followed immediately by even more strident, parodistic march music for snare drum, horns, trumpets, and eventually the full wind section (with squealing piccolo). The entry of pizzicato cellos and basses signals a gradual return to calm, with quiet solo timpani and soft violins bringing this episode to a close.

Scene 3 (Meno mosso [slower]): Three loud brass chords conjure up a wandering dialogue between upper and lower strings, joined by piccolo, then flutes, and finally arriving at a lovely passage for strings alone.

Scene 4 (Allegro): One of Shostakovich's burlesque scherzos, including chattering woodwinds and xylophone. The brass contribute some circus music of their own as well. Cymbals and glockenspiel introduce a jolly theme in rising three-note phrases that gradually takes over the texture. The tempo slows a bit as the strings attempt a more serious and stately utterance for a few moments, and then the full orchestra unites over a snare-drum roll in a series of broad pronouncements that collapse into thuds on the bass drum (which has the final word).

Scene 5 (Andante, then Largo): A truly weird episode led off by solo tuba, interspersed with gruff *glissandos* (slides) on lower strings, a couple of loud crashes on the tam-tam, and recitatives from solo brass. A *recitative* is simply a musical stylization of actual speech. It's exactly what Beethoven gives to his cellos and basses at the opening of the finale of the Ninth Symphony. Here, the argument grows in intensity and culminates in a cymbal crash.

Scene 6 (Chorus): Introduced by the strings, the concluding chorus uses a poem that is, if possible, even worse than the one at the end of the Second Symphony: "With factories and colonies marching in the May Day parade, we will harvest the land, our time has come. Listen, Proletariat, to the sound of the factories. As you incinerate the old you rekindle the new reality . . . " etc, ad nauseam. It kind of makes you long for the old reality, but never mind. Like its companion in the Second Symphony, Shostakovich gets through it with a minimum of fuss and bother, albeit a maximum of volume. The ideological point thus emphatically made, the symphony marches glowingly into the future, trumpets well to the fore. It's no masterpiece, not by a long shot, but it's also not as bad as some would have us believe.

Piano Concerto No. 1
1933

Orchestration: solo piano, solo trumpet, strings

The chronology of Shostakovich's works reveals that quite a bit had been happening between the Third Symphony and this piano concerto:

The Flea (incidental music) (1929)
The Golden Age (ballet) (1930)
The Bolt (ballet) (1930–31)
Alone (film score) (1931)
Hypothetically Murdered (incidental music) (1931)
Golden Hills (film score) (1931)
Rule, Britannia (incidental music) (1931)
Hamlet (incidental music) (1931–32)
Lady Macbeth of Mtsensk District (opera) (1930–32)
Passer-by (film score) (1932)
The Counterplan (film score) (1932)
24 Preludes for Piano (1932–33)

He was now a professional composer in full command of his mature style, having abandoned a possible career as a concert pianist back in 1927. His operatic masterpiece, *Lady Macbeth of Mtsensk District,* was successfully launched, and he had made important contributions to stage, screen, and the dance. The experience of working on these various theatrical scores matters because they allowed Shostakovich to develop one of his most telling gifts: that of parody. Combined with his experience as a cinema pianist and knowledge of operetta, he quickly learned to spice his music with a wicked sense of humor, a quality frequently derided and misunderstood, particularly when it characterizes supposedly "serious" works such as symphonies and concertos.

More than merely indulging in comedy, however, the aforementioned works mark a return to music based on clear-cut melody, on the structural use of tonality, and also to a growing awareness on Shostakovich's part (especially in the opera) of his role as a Russian artist, as part of a great musical tradition. The result is an extremely rich and diverse musical language, and one moreover that is also quite often emotionally ambivalent, as may be expected when humorous and serious elements rub shoulders within the same movement or work. In short, Shostakovich was never a stylistically "pure" composer, like Brahms or Mozart. He was an eclectic, like Haydn and Mahler, and like them, his personal idiom consists of a wide range of melodic archetypes, consistently used and quite specific in meaning. You can hear this very clearly in the First Piano Concerto, which he wrote for his own use (and also recorded).

First Movement: Allegretto–Allegro vivace

With a flourish from the piano and muted trumpet (remember the muted trumpet opening of the First Symphony), the soloist launches the concerto with a soulful minor-key tune clearly founded on the first measures of Beethoven's "Appassionata" Sonata. This movement uses a sophisticated combination of sonata and rondo form, and has the shape AB–development–ACA. The first subject (the ritornello of the rondo), begun by the soloist, continues in the violins and leads to a vigorous transition in dialogue between piano and strings. Shostakovich takes special care to highlight the arrival of the contrasting second subject (the first episode of the rondo), not just thematically, but also using tempo and timbre. The speed increases to Allegro vivace; the mood turns comic, the key gleefully major; and shortly thereafter, the trumpet reappears for the first time since the opening measures. You may note a resemblance between the trumpet's melody and that of the cat in Prokofiev's *Peter and the Wolf,* which was actually written three years later.

The development section tosses all this material together like a salad, in vivid exchanges between the piano, trumpet, and strings. It reaches a climax with one last blast from the trumpet of its "cat" theme, before settling down to the initial allegretto tempo and a return to the first subject, hinted at by the piano but continued in regular fashion by the violins. Shostakovich reveals his newly found formal creativity, as well as the flexibility of his mature language, when he arrives once again at the second subject—this time a plain allegro, in which the same type of music returns (that is, rhythmic and in the style of comic operetta)—but the trumpet does not participate, and the actual tunes are different. This C episode gives the movement a wonderful feeling of freshness and a nicely improvisatory quality but also a perfectly balanced array of content. The quiet close, for which Shostakovich has reserved the piano's opening theme (now accompanied by long, low notes on the trumpet), gives the necessary feeling of finality.

Although brief, this movement accomplishes quite a bit in a small space (five to six minutes on average). The ensuing slow movement is entirely serious in tone, the finale wholly comic, but this opening is both and so establishes the emotional polarity at the very heart of the concerto right from the beginning. It defines the music's expressive dimensions, just as often happens in the great works of the classical masters (Haydn, Mozart, and Beethoven). Shostakovich's use of thematic archetypes in the second subject effectively enlarges the listener's subjective perception of the movement's very compact form, while at the same time enhancing the element of surprise and eliminating the need for literal repetition. These are all ideas that will serve Shostakovich very well in the works to come.

Second Movement: Lento

This lovely movement is a slow waltz, led off by muted strings, later joined and extended by solo piano, and then continued by both solo and orchestra together. The form of this piece is a simple ABA, with the B section consisting of a passionate interlude largely for solo piano, with some sharp interjections from the strings, culminating in a single pizzicato *plink* from the violins, violas, and cellos, backed by the piano. When the waltz returns, it's played in a haunting, bluesy variation by muted solo trumpet. Some commentators hear a resemblance between this passage and the trumpet solo in the slow movement of Gershwin's Concerto in F (1825), while the bittersweet waltz itself also recalls the central movement of Ravel's Concerto in G Major (1932).

Both here and in the finale, the "French Connection" is very much to the point, for Russia's nineteenth-century musical culture was essentially French in its orientation towards ballet, opera, exotic subjects, and orchestral brilliance. The elements that Shostakovich borrowed from this Gallic wellspring were not wholly flattering to their source, since he seemed to associate them principally with Offenbachian frivolity and superficiality, while at the same time respecting the fastidiousness and craftsmanship characteristic of the French aesthetic. The seminal work in this case is the silent film score *The New Babylon,* set in late nineteenth-century Paris, which afforded Shostakovich the opportunity to run amok, musically speaking, in lampooning the sort of French music purportedly symbolic of "bourgeois decadence." He universalized this idiom in the ballet *The Golden Age,* and the rest, as they say, is history.

Third Movement: Moderato
Finale: Allegro con brio

The third movement serves as prelude to the fourth. It rhapsodizes romantically as piano and strings share a couple of minutes of passionate reverie. Led off by a short cadenza for the soloist, the violins take up a lovely melody that could serve as the subject for an entire movement all by itself. The music becomes steadily dreamier, piano and high strings engaged in a sweet duet, until a brief hesitation and a sprightly run up the keyboard launch the finale. This is another rondo, but a simpler one than the first movement, with no distinct development section. In this particular case, there are two episodes followed by a coda, and so the movement has this shape: ABACA–coda.

Violins present the initial rondo theme, or ritornello, a jolly idea full of repeated notes, not to mention French insouciance. If you know the contemporaneous works of Parisian composer Francis Poulenc, you'll recognize the music-hall, tongue-in-cheek ambiance immediately. Solo piano begins the first episode (B), a loony succession of tunes culminating in an insane, presto gallop with prominent trumpet fanfares. Notice the faint whiff of Rossini's *William Tell* overture: Shostakovich was virtually obsessed by the rhythm of its "Lone Ranger" dash to the finish, even to the point of quoting it literally in the first movement of the Fifteenth Symphony.

A very skillfully managed transition leads to an abbreviated statement of the ritornello, this time by the piano. Episode C is a tipsy trumpet solo, accompanied by the dry clicking of strings struck with the wooden backs of their bows (*col legno*). The ritornello sails in once again, on the violins as at the beginning, and then Shostakovich offers a two-part coda, consisting of a manic cadenza for the pianist that immediately ignites a hilarious comic windup. This is none other than the crazy gallop from the movement's B episode, and it brings the concerto to a brilliant and zany conclusion in satisfyingly punctual fashion.

Part 3

Middle-Period Works

Symphony No. 4
1935–36

Orchestration: 2 piccolos, 4 flutes, 4 oboes, English horn, E-flat clarinet, 4 clarinets, bass clarinet, 3 bassoons, contrabassoon, 4 trumpets, 8 horns, 3 trombones, 2 tubas, 2 sets of timpani, triangle, snare drum, bass drum, cymbals, tam-tam, xylophone, glockenspiel, woodblock, castanets, celesta, two harps, strings

The Fourth Symphony is a massive juggernaut of a piece, requiring a huge orchestra, and very unconventional in form. It's the exact opposite of the neoclassical kind of writing that you hear in the First Piano Concerto. This is music that rises to the Mahlerian challenge of writing a symphony that "embraces everything," a world unto itself. In short, it's a hyper-romantic piece, larger than life but at the same time antiheroic in outlook. Every one of its three large movements ends quietly, in an atmosphere of mystery, neither happy nor sad but with a profound sense of "otherness," in a realm that exists beyond human emotion.

Given its self-contained originality, it's not surprising that Shostakovich withdrew the work from rehearsal after the first attacks appeared against him in *Pravda*. If *Lady Macbeth of Mtsensk District* had created a scandal, then this would quite literally have put his very life at risk. And yet the music, while often deafeningly loud and dissonant, is easy to follow, full of memorable ideas and tunes, and very convincing as it stands. Shostakovich fans have a special fondness for the piece. Some commentators, as well as the composer himself, have suggested that this is more the kind of thing he would have continued doing had he considered it safe. On the other hand, the music fairly bristles with those increasingly traditional elements of harmony and melody that he would go on to develop throughout his career, so in that sense, the argument is moot. What matters is that this remains one of his most distinctive symphonies, not that he didn't go on to produce more of the same.

First Movement: Allegretto poco moderato

The form of this huge movement, lasting nearly half an hour, is actually incredibly simple in its basic outlines: ABABA. One of the invariable practices that great composers often follow is the rule that the larger (that is, longer) the movement, the simpler the form. This is because anything that takes up a great deal of time needs to consist of very memorable thematic ideas if the listener is to follow the argument as it unfolds. All the contrasts need to be maximized. At the same time, in order to avoid monotony, Shostakovich takes care to minimize literal repetition in the sense that no tune is ever played by the exact same instrument, or combination of instruments, more than once. He achieves a remarkable amount of variety by constantly varying the scoring, rhythm, accompaniments, and tempo at which the principal themes appear.

Part of the movement's fundamental dichotomy of ideas stems from the fact that A is a march and B is a waltz, a situation very similar to what you heard in the first movement of the First Symphony, only on a much larger scale. Each section lasts around five minutes, give or take, whenever it appears, and contains subsidiary ideas as well, so don't expect the music to adhere

Symphony No. 4

to some pedantically strict formal outline. When Shostakovich wants you to recognize a variation of one of the main themes, you will without difficulty. Otherwise, simply enjoy the impression of profuse variety, secure in the knowledge that the more familiar with it you become, the more you will hear. This music has what you might call "deep content"–great staying power that rewards repetition, assuming that your neighbors don't complain and you have the time.

Section A: As you heard in connection with the first movement of Piano Concerto No. 1, Shostakovich likes working with certain melodic or thematic archetypes, and this frees him from the need to repeat tunes literally or even at all. So when I say that this is a "march," what this really means is "march music" generally. It can be identified by the melody, but also by mere rhythm or even the scoring. In other words, a musical "idea" need not always be the actual theme but any other sonic aspect of the piece. Like many of Shostakovich's first subjects, whether or not they turn up in sonata-form movements, this one subdivides into a sort of mini-rondo: abaca. The "a" bits are the most noisy and marchlike, while the two episodes offer contrasting material that tries but fails to establish something of a different character.

Brittle trills on woodwinds and xylophone, topped by suspended cymbal crashes, launch the initial strident march, blasted out by the brass against a stubborn repeated-note accompaniment. The music is deliberately crude and rises quickly to a huge climax with assistance from the bass drum and tam-tam, with high horns and whiplike chords on brass and woodwinds. A contrasting, more lyrical idea follows in the strings, interspersed by bits of march: repeated-note figures, soft snare-drum riffs, and fragments of brass fanfares. This leads back to a varied restatement of the opening, even louder and more powerfully sustained, grindingly dissonant and mocking in tone (lots of cackling xylophone), ending at last with the same high horn fanfare as previously.

The next section (c) begins with chuckling woodwinds in triplet rhythms interrupted by isolated plucked-string chords, underpinned by repeated timpani beats. As the entire woodwind section puts together a few sardonic phrases, the timpani rhythm begins to skip along impishly, but before this gets established for any length of time, pleading strings interrupt with a very short but passionate lament that rushes to the loudest and most chaotic climax yet heard. This cuts off as quickly as it erupted, bringing the movement's opening A section to its close.

Section B: This particular waltz often has a limp, in the form of dropped and added beats that upset the basic triple-time rhythm. It begins on the solo bassoon, very lightly accompanied by pizzicato cellos and basses, flecks of harp, and occasional woodwind solos. Cellos and violas, then violins, continue the melody and extend it wistfully. Shostakovich then passes the tune to the bass clarinet, against delicate repeated notes in the harp. Diaphanous string chords separate this statement from the next one, begun by solo horn and leading (after a couple of short digressions) to this section's principal climax. On its other side, two tubas belch out the waltz grotesquely against vicious two-note slaps from various winds, brass, and percussion. This grim vision is interrupted by:

Section A: The entire woodwind section, sometimes joined by sneering brass and pizzicato strings, plays a comical variation on the opening march. This trips along for a couple of minutes in jocular fashion, until the violins race off with the fugue from hell, an insane whirlwind of counterpoint (a *fugue* is similar to a round, in which each musical voice plays the same music, in staggered entries but on different notes of the

Symphony No. 4

scale). One string section after the other enters, with the fugue subject played so quickly that its individual notes are practically indistinguishable. As the intensity increases, the counterpoint comes together in a galloping rhythm immediately taken over by timpani, woodblock, bass drum, and snare drum. Horns belt out the march tune in long notes, and as the rest of the brass join in, cymbals and tam-tam provoke a cataclysm of truly epic proportions. The accumulated energy gets discharged as strings continue the opening march, the texture gradually thinning out until the music surprisingly morphs into:

Section B: A surprisingly graceful return to the waltz, elegantly poised in the violins. This passes once again to the bass clarinet, then to lower strings remarkably accompanied by flutter-tongued *tremolos* (rapidly repeated notes) on the four flutes. An ominous series of eight crescendos, beginning on solo timpani and increasing in volume and density, introduces what seems like a return to the symphony's opening gesture. The music is only slightly varied, but as the strings stomp along, the tune that they accompany isn't the march at all but the waltz, in muted brass. Its continuation, on solo English horn, then solo violin, represents the fullest statement of this idea since it was first heard, even though the music is completely rescored. As the solo violin subsides, along with isolated notes on the harps, the bass drum softly takes up the march rhythm, leading to:

Section A: This last appearance features a solo bassoon, assisted by the English horn, in a complete statement of the entire march idea (just as B above offered the entire waltz). It sounds singularly glum and grumpy in its naked simplicity, bereft of its intimidating volume and brass sonorities—truly a case of Shostakovich at his Shakespearian best, revealing his crude march to be (as you might have suspected all along) a tale told by an idiot, full of sound and fury, signifying nothing. After a last flourish from the woodwinds and a sudden upwelling from the harps, soft tam-tam strokes cushion the music as it sinks into darkness.

Second Movement: Moderato con moto

This scherzo has a form that should now be familiar to you: ABABA, only on a much smaller scale than the preceding movement and with minimal variations in melody that make the form much easier to follow. The opening section alternates statements of the main theme—with its four-note initial motive, first from the strings, then the woodwinds—leading to a climax for full orchestra (minus heavy percussion). The melody has a cool, nonchalant quality that will also characterize the slowish scherzos of the Seventh (second movement), Tenth (third movement), and Fifteenth (third movement) symphonies.

Solo timpani bang out a couple of loud two-note phrases, and the B section begins with a gentle theme based on a descending scale, accompanied by a soft galloping rhythm. It bears a very close family resemblance to what will become the principal subjects of the Fifth Symphony's first movement. As with the A section, this new melody begins on the violins but gets taken over by the woodwinds (and solo horn). Solo timpani also round off this section, now with a loud three-note motive.

The return of A is a very large-scale fugue, and here the strings/winds polarization is even stronger than previously. Shostakovich divides the fugue into two parts: the first entirely for strings, the second entirely for winds (all the flutes and clarinets initially). As more and more winds join in, this fugue rolls into a loud restatement of section B on the horns, while the rest of the woodwinds have the moderate galloping rhythm. The entry of the full string section doubling the woodwinds signals the gradual return of A, this time hypnotically accompanied by a tick-tock rhythmic pattern on woodblock, snare drum, and castanets. This marvelously eerie sonority will return at the end of the Second Cello Concerto and the Fifteenth Symphony.

Third Movement: Largo

Although it begins slowly, like the first movement, this finale goes through a large number of changes in tempo. The sequence of events is:

Slow Funeral March (A)
Quick Toccata (B)
Dance Suite (A varied): Moderate Waltz–Burlesque/Gallop–
   Quick Waltz
Moderate Toccata (B varied)
Slow Funeral March (Chorale) (A varied, with coda)

The music of this finale is the most colorful of all, and its dance orientation ensures that most of it is quite catchy, melodically as well as rhythmically. Also, since the central dance suite is actually a miniature set of variations on the opening funeral march, it's also reasonable to view the form of this movement as ABABA—exactly the same as the previous two movements—even though the variation format and avoidance of literal repetition tends to conceal the music's underlying symmetry. Still, the subconscious impression of formal balance remains strong, and this type of structure isn't as unusual as it seems: Shostakovich would do something similar on a slightly smaller scale in the Sixth Symphony, which also has three movements of very different character, all sharing the same basic form. Now consider each section a bit more closely.

Slow Funeral March

The prowling opening theme reveals Shostakovich at his most Mahlerian, and calls attention to the fact that this is his first use of the contrabassoon in a symphony. He quickly grew to love its dark, gruff timbre, and the trio of two bassoons plus contrabassoon will characterize many passages in later works. Take special care to notice the first entrance of the oboe: its haunting, three-note rising motive, similar to the one that opens the march, generates most of the thematic material that follows. This section rises to a blazing major-key climax, with blaring trumpets, before subsiding into its original gloom. Chains of warbling oboes effect the transition to the next section.

Quick Toccata

The word *toccata* comes from the Italian, meaning "to touch" or play an instrument, specifically one with a keyboard. In Bach's day, this meant a written-out improvisation, crystallizing the kinds of things a performer might do to try out a new instrument. There would be rapid scales and flourishes, interspersed with runs up and down the keyboard, all designed to help the player get familiar with the organ or harpsichord's strengths and weaknesses. In later music, as conceived for orchestra, the term simply means a sort of perpetual-motion piece in steady rhythm, and that's exactly what Shostakovich delivers. He was fond of this type of texture: it appears in many of his later symphonies, most famously as the third movement of the Eighth.

Because the entire point of the music is an emphasis on steady rhythm and rapid motion, the music is athematic; focus instead on how the rhythmic patterns get broken up and tossed from one section to the next in an ever-changing kaleidoscope of musical shapes. At the central climax, Shostakovich does offer an actual tune, and a brilliant one at that, on violins with a prominent glockenspiel part. This tune, after its initial rising phrase, features a chain of descending three-note sequences, and these gradually take over the toccata entirely, bringing it to a full stop against sustained notes in the horns. Some chirpy woodwind motives in polka rhythm lead to the:

Dance Suite: Moderate Waltz

Although it begins on cellos backed by harps, the actual waltz rhythm takes firm shape when flutes and violins get a hold on the tune. The only word to describe this music is *succulent*. The tonality is surprisingly unclouded by dissonance: indeed, it sounds as if this music could have been written a century previously, and if Shostakovich's intention is parody, then it's an affectionate one. Every so often the dance looses its footing, and the textures threaten to thin out alarmingly, but the overall impression of good-natured charm remains pretty firmly in place.

Burlesque/Gallop

This delightful bit of parody begins on solo bassoon with a drunken tune whose derivation from the opening funeral march is relatively easy to hear. Each presentation of this tune concludes with a catchy refrain from the full string section. Various episodes separate the recurrences of this theme, including one that features an overly optimistic solo trombone, until the music finally manages to put together a consistent gallop rhythm. This leads directly into the next section.

Quick Waltz

Pizzicato strings accompany what starts out as a trio featuring flute, clarinet, and bassoon. Other members of the same families join in, as does that boisterous trombone from the previous section, tending to cut across the waltz rhythm. This brief episode segues smoothly into the:

Moderate Toccata

This toccata is entirely for strings in steady duple meter, until the very end when once again the solo trombone makes a brief appearance. Long, soft woodwind chords underpinned by steady beats in the cellos and basses introduce a transition passage featuring broad string phrases, a tiny recollection of the first waltz, and a rumbling *ostinato* (repeated rhythmic figure) in the lower strings.

Slow Funeral March (Chorale)

As the ostinato slows to a halt, the two timpanists start a new one, and with a huge crescendo, the funeral march returns in the form of a loud, dissonant brass chorale, reaching skywards. It's supposed to be heroic, but the notes are all wrong, and the result is unsettling. This moves from one cymbal-capped, tam-tam-led climax to the next, always urged on by the pounding timpani and thudding bass drum, with the oboe phrase from the movement's opening shrieked out by the full woodwind section. A last crash on the tam-tam causes the chorale to self-destruct, and the final few minutes of the symphony are coda. Over the

Symphony No. 4

persistent, pulsing note C in timpani, low harps, and double basses, that pungent oboe motive appears for the last time in muted trumpet, while strings sustain the final chord for pages on end, and the celesta coldly repeats a rocking figure, a symbol of infinite, empty space.

This mysterious, timeless coda is the very antithesis of what the Soviet authorities would have demanded of Shostakovich in 1936, and it's no surprise that under the circumstances he withdrew the symphony (it was premiered in 1961). But many such eerie open endings would follow: indeed, the first movement of the Fifth Symphony finishes quite similarly, celesta and all. Negating the conventional triumphant apotheosis and leaving listeners with a musical question mark may not be the conclusion that the strident initial gesture of this massive work seems to promise, but taken on its own, it is without a doubt disturbingly beautiful and somehow, inexplicably, exactly right.

Symphony No. 6
1939

Orchestration: piccolo, 2 flutes, 2 oboes, English horn, E-flat clarinet, 3 clarinets, bass clarinet, 3 bassoons, contrabassoon, 3 trumpets, 4 horns, 3 trombones, tuba, timpani, triangle, snare drum, bass drum, cymbals, tam-tam, xylophone, tambourine, celesta, harp, strings

It's always amusing to see commentators accusing Shostakovich of "selling out" in writing the Fifth Symphony, only to express puzzlement at the special features of his subsequent essays in the genre. The Sixth offers a case in point. Beginning with an enormous slow movement followed by two short, quick ones, its form has caused a certain amount of confusion. Shostakovich certainly realized that there is more to musical originality than a trendy avant-garde style featuring a high level of relative dissonance. Accordingly, the Sixth is one of his most interesting creations, but it's also one of his most approachable and appealing. It's a very underappreciated aspect of Shostakovich's greatness that he had the ability to be both true to his art and kind to his listeners.

Unfortunately, many artists and critics of a more misanthropic bent denigrate this sort of aesthetic humanism, but this matters not a bit. Once you know the symphony well, the beauty and simplicity of its design will become increasingly evident. It follows a totally convincing emotional progression from darkness and desolation, to bittersweet humor tinged with nostalgia, to rambunctious high spirits, and does so in about half an hour. The result is fresh sounding, never overly taxing, and at the same time satisfyingly complete, both formally and expressively.

One useful fact worth noting about this symphony is that all three of its movements have exactly the same shape: ABAB, a.k.a. "sonata form without a development section." This does not mean that there is no sense of progress to the musical argument. On the contrary, there's plenty, because restatements of important thematic material are always recomposed and varied in melody, phrase length, volume, and scoring. In each movement, the difference between the first (A) and second (B) subjects is not just a matter of the actual melodies but also of the contrast between a predominance of triple versus duple rhythms (whether in terms of the actual time signature or simply the way the music is notated).

First Movement	Second Movement	Third Movement
A (triple) (minor)	A (triple) (major)	A (duple) (minor)
B (duple) (minor)	B (duple) (minor)	B (triple) (major)

Furthermore, all of the duple-rhythm ("in two" or march-type) tunes throughout the symphony are subtly related by shared motives, and the same is true of the triple-time ("in three") themes. If this isn't obvious at first listening, don't worry, because it's not supposed to be. Shostakovich, like all great composers, understood that these procedures don't have to be academically strict. What matters is creating a subconscious feeling of coherence when listening, and for this purpose, the mere suggestion of similarity is just as important (indeed, often more so) than any emphatic point making.

Note also the balance of tonalities (major vs. minor). As you can see, the second and third movements are mirror images of each other, arranged so that the major (happy) ending prevails at the conclusion of the symphony. Shostakovich gives this process an even greater feeling of inevitability by having the repeat of the B section progressively grow in size from one movement to the next. In the first movement, it's a tiny reminiscence only a few bars long. In the central scherzo, the second subject returns in full; while in the finale, it gets repeated, developed, and extended into a lengthy coda. So even though the first movement is almost wholly dark and longer than the other two movements combined, there's more than enough contrast in mood to balance its depth of sadness, and the emotional progression from despair to joy is very skillfully plotted.

First Movement: Largo

The opening of the Sixth Symphony combines the tragic grandeur of the Fifth Symphony's first movement with the slow tempo of that work's own largo. Although written in what's known as *common time* (that is, four beats to the measure), the principal theme for the most part flows along to a steady accompaniment in triplets (three notes in the space of two) and frequently breaks into triplet motion itself. This has the effect of minimizing the impression of slow march tempo, and it gives the music a singing quality that greatly enhances its expressivity. There are two motives that turn out to be important in the rest of the symphony: the first four notes of the whole work (and their rhythm) and the seven-note motive that you hear in the violins at the first entrance of the timpani. This consists of three rising notes, a longer note (usually trilled), and then another three-note rising motive. It becomes a kind of refrain between the successively evolving statements of the longer main theme.

After the passionate opening exordium, the music settles down to one of Shostakovich's characteristic laments, first on violins, gradually taken over the full woodwind section, then desolately whistled by the piccolo with delicate touches of color from the harp. A last return of the seven-note "refrain" motive on English horn precedes a searing climax in which the trumpet screams out the movement's opening phrase while strings stride downwards in a series of evil-sounding trills. Timpani pound out the rhythm "dum, dadum," and the French horns blast out a baleful tune that imposes an uneasy calm over the rest of the orchestra. The volume slowly ebbs until nothing is left but trilling violins and soft two-note fragments in timpani, plucked cellos, and basses—and later, low harp. This is the empty, frozen landscape that the B section inhabits.

It begins with a solo English horn (an instrument with a lot to do in this movement), offering a tiny motive consisting largely of the climactic timpani rhythm just heard, which in fact forms the basis for much of this section and gives it a funeral-march-like character. From this small musical seed, Shostakovich spins out a sad melody, followed by muted trumpets with another variant of the funereal rhythm. Remember this simple motive: it will generate the galloping opening theme of the presto finale. Next comes a flute solo, full of simple pathos, until the violins take over and lead to a tragic climax before subsiding once again into stillness. Notice how the omnipresence of that simple "dum, dadum" rhythm permits Shostakovich to present his themes without literal repetition, while still making it clear that they all belong to the same family.

On the other side of the central climax, clarinets now have the muted trumpet rhythm, followed by even more fragmentary bits of melody from oboe, English horn, and very soft violins. A gentle stroke on the tam-tam introduces yet another flute solo, soon a duet, the two instruments warbling like lone birds in a haunted musical wasteland. A short interlude on the violins ends with another soft tam-tam stroke plus a reminder of the A section's seven-note motive from the symphony's beginning, before the flutes take over once more. In its only appearance in the entire symphony, Shostakovich gives the celesta the violins' continuous trill, and into this eerie stillness, a solo horn injects a note of desperately needed warmth in a major key, ending once again with the seven-note motive. This time, the A section actually returns, preserving some of the same warmth, now meltingly lyrical and consoling.

The relief, however, turns out to be short lived. The texture thins and dissolves in a wave of triplets from the bass clarinet, as solo bassoon mournfully returns to a last, brief recollection of the funeral-march rhythm of B. Muted violins, soft timpani beats doubled by the harp in its lowest register, and gentle string chords bring the movement to its conclusion. This is music beyond sadness: "numb" more properly describes it, a mere hovering on the edge of feeling. It's an unforgettable ending to one of Shostakovich's most elegiac and beautiful movements. From this point on, the symphony's mood will grow progressively lighter.

Second Movement: Allegro

Although the tempo of this movement is quick and the music full of that tipsy woodwind writing characteristic of Shostakovich's fast scherzos—witness the First, Eighth, and Ninth symphonies, as well as the second movement of the First Violin Concerto—the mood here is bittersweet, with an especially well-judged mixture of major and minor modes. A solo clarinet leads off, to a simple accompaniment that establishes the triple-time rhythm. It's actually quite a while before a clear tune breaks in, following the first cymbal crash and after a downward sweep from the strings and woodwinds, backed by the harp. When it finally arrives, this rising theme on horns answered by fanfares from the trumpets and xylophone turns out to be a variation on the symphony's opening phrase. Compare the rhythm of the first four notes of each tune, and you'll catch the similarity immediately.

The music after this first climax is reflective, with solos for bass clarinet and flute, lightly accompanied by harp, leading gently to the more vigorous middle section, based on B of the first movement. Once again, note the rhythmic similarities between the main motives in each case and the way that Shostakovich emphasizes the theme's duple rhythm, here cutting across the music's basic triple time. The shape of this new melody is quite memorable, with heavily accented "yelps" at the end of each phrase. A very similar idea will characterize the middle section of the Second Cello Concerto's scherzo as well. Building itself up in layers throughout the orchestra, moving from winds, to strings, to low brass, the tune becomes increasingly militant and marchlike as it progresses. It reaches a climax featuring a violently trilling return to the A section's brass fanfare—capped by a tam-tam crash and a big ritard that, with a mighty thwack on the bass drum, snaps like a rubber band and launches a virtuoso timpani solo.

The return to the opening music is marvelous: flute and bass clarinet play the tune normally and in a simultaneous mirror image (or inversion). The piccolo also strikes up with a wistfully chirping theme full of broken phrases and scales, echoed by other members of the woodwind family. Under the steady, gently galloping accompaniment of the strings, the main theme of the B section now returns, at length. The music has a captivating, twilit ambience that gradually grows calmer and darker, until with a sudden upward run on woodwinds and harp, and a delicate tap on the xylophone, the music vanishes like the popping of a soap bubble. Shostakovich is not often a composer lauded for his elegance and grace, but these were qualities in which he was actually very strong, nowhere more so than in this finesse-filled scherzo.

Third Movement: Presto

The finale is a gallop in Shostakovich's patented faux-operetta style, complete with a "*William Tell* overture" opening theme deriving from B of the first movement, and also bearing a striking resemblance to a sequence from the film score *Volachayev Days* (1937). Whatever the actual tempo that the conductor chooses for this presto, it's critical that it sound quicker than the preceding movement, an effect achieved as much through crisp, light articulation as through speed. The strings, in particular, need to display some serious virtuosity in order to do the music full justice. In keeping with his frequent practice, Shostakovich presents the main theme as a sort of mini-rondo in verse-and-refrain form. It keeps returning to the beginning, like a puppy chasing its own tail. Between these returns to the opening gallop, Shostakovich presents a series of humorous little episodes, including one that sounds suspiciously like a send-up of the finale of Mozart's famous 40th Symphony in G minor (K. 550).

After a couple of minutes of this musical game of tag, the contrasting section begins with a switch to triple time rumbling in the lower strings. The tune is related to that seven-note motive from the first movement's A section—the one with three-note rising phrases on either side of a trill. Here it's those rising phrases that both have in common, although the trill also puts in a humorous appearance independently on the woodwinds. As in the previous movement, this central section builds to a huge climax, with timpani fanfares and a big crash on the tam-tam, before the bass drum thumps the orchestra into submission and a solo bassoon sings a curiously oriental-sounding bit of melody (shades of the scherzo of the First Symphony).

Shortly thereafter, a violin solo winds its way back to the opening theme one last time. This recapitulation is designed so as to make the switch from the initial minor key to a breezy major.

The entry of the triangle signals the change: you can't miss it. As the high spirits rise, the B section returns, also modified, in the form of circus music on the horns. Woodwinds and violins strike up a vivacious march accompanied by quiet percussion (bass drum, cymbals, and triangle), leading to an uproarious comic windup as the circus music takes a few final bows, between which timpani interject emphatic applause. The final bars are as happy and carefree as anything that Shostakovich ever wrote, but also about as far as possible from the heroically serious perorations demanded by the tenets of Socialist Realism. Clearly Shostakovich wasn't content with doing more of the same after the success of the Fifth, but the emotional journey traveled over the course of the Sixth is nevertheless just as wide and just as convincingly articulated, no matter how unorthodox the overall form.

Symphony No. 7 ("Leningrad")

1941

Orchestration: piccolo, 3 flutes, alto flute, 2 oboes, English horn, E-flat clarinet, 3 clarinets, bass clarinet, 2 bassoons, contrabassoon, 6 trumpets, 8 horns, 6 trombones, tuba, timpani, triangle, 3 snare drums, bass drum, cymbals, tam-tam, xylophone, tambourine, 2 harps, piano, strings

Given the discussions about the expressive intentions of some of Shostakovich's finales, it's nice to see a work with a controversial first movement instead. The title of this symphony comes from the dedication: "To the City of Leningrad," the composer's birthplace. Whether you accept the party line on this symphony or not, no one has yet questioned the sincerity of this dedication or Shostakovich's genuine love for either his country or his childhood home. The date is also significant: wartime, and the Nazi blockade of Leningrad, an episode of appalling human suffering and great hardship, as well as courage and self-sacrifice. Shostakovich himself worked as a volunteer fireman before being evacuated to the safety of the countryside, where he completed this symphony.

And yet, despite moments of darkness (mostly in the second half of the first movement), this symphony is one of his sunniest works. It begins in an unclouded C major tonality. The scherzo is twilit in its outer sections, boisterous and cheerful in the middle, and certainly never miserable. Likewise the slow movement: it's solemn and passionate, to be sure, alternately heroic and lyrical, with plenty of emotional intensity but little suffering and no despair. And while the finale begins in darkness, it quickly launches a vigorous, very Russian initial allegro, which subsides into a solemn interlude before building to the inevitably triumphant conclusion. There's very little of the Fifth's desolation, that haunted emptiness you can also hear in the first movement of the previous symphony and that will feature so prominently in the next one. In fact, there are many ways to look at this piece. Perhaps the music itself will tell us more.

First Movement: Allegretto

This movement surely is *not* about marching Nazis. I am quite amazed that anyone could ever have thought so, even during wartime, even after a superficial first hearing. The very idea is nonsense. Music is powerless to express "the threat of fascism," and it would be even weirder had Shostakovich chosen to do it as here, by taking a simple, innocuous tune and blowing it up to monstrous proportions. These must be the least threatening Nazis in musical history! By the same token, I have very strong doubts about the music being about "the Leningrad that Stalin destroyed and that Hitler merely finished off." So claims Solomon Volkov in *Testimony,* the book that purports to be Shostakovich's memoirs. That makes just as little sense in considering a work that is optimistic not only at its end but pretty much throughout. This doesn't mean that the piece is free of conflict—far from it—but its tensions are not demonstrably specific to any particular time or evocative of a specific place.

It so happens that other comments of the composer's have been preserved, and they prove considerably more enlightening. They can be found in Elizabeth Wilson's excellent collection

Shostakovich: A Life Remembered. Wilson cites the recollection of Flora Litvinova, a close family friend of the composer who was actually present when he completed the symphony and played through it at the piano for the first time. After the performance, while drinking tea with Shostakovich and his wife, Litvinova records him as saying: "Of course—Fascism. But music, real music, can never be literally tied to a theme. National Socialism is not the only form of Fascism; this music is about all forms of terror, slavery, the bondage of the spirit." A few paragraphs later she adds another revealing comment: "For Shostakovich nothing was more hateful than vulgar banality." This is an observation confirmed by many others that knew him.

Let me now propose an experiment. Assume that the first movement does indeed express "the bondage of the spirit" and does so in a purely musical way, symbolized by that "vulgar banality" that Shostakovich found so hateful. The question then becomes: How does the form serve the content of this movement in order to convey its theoretically self-evident emotional meaning? Can "real music," as Shostakovich used the term, do such a thing? I believe that it can and does. Here's how.

The symphony opens with a sturdy theme in the strings, immediately repeated by the woodwinds. It strides up and down the scale with wide melodic leaps, a constantly shifting center of tonal gravity, and freely changing time signatures, like a march with a tendency to trip over itself in its unbuttoned enthusiasm. Two memorable motives are critically important: first, the rhythm in trumpets and drums after the first eight notes (dum, dadadum), which for ease of identification I will simply call the Rhythm, with a capital *R*. Next, about a minute or so in, there's a second solo passage for the woodwind section, consisting of two descending four-note phrases separated by string fanfares incorporating the Rhythm. These short woodwind phrases both end with two emphatic repeated notes.

If you identify and remember this pair of ideas, which Shostakovich takes care to highlight for you, then you hold the key to much of the subsequent action. After the second of them appears, the music calms down rapidly, and the long, lyrical second subject begins in the violins, smoother and more flowing than the opening. It leads to a woodwind refrain featuring three chiming, repeated chords (shades of the slow movement of Tchaikovsky's Fourth Symphony). Lower strings take over the melody, leading once again to the refrain (in the violins and flute this time). Stillness settles over the orchestra, as piccolo and then solo violin spin out a couple of lines of dreamy melody and draw the exposition section to a close. It only takes about six minutes, making it proportionally one of Shostakovich's shortest.

This means that given the nearly thirty-minute length of the movement, the development section will necessarily be his longest, if not to say most notorious. As the snare drum taps out a steady military rhythm in a gradual crescendo, the orchestra plays a tacky little tune twelve times, adding instruments on each repetition, rather like Ravel's *Boléro* (1928), which was hardly the ubiquitous warhorse in 1941 that it later became. Each repetition is separated by a ten-note refrain, divided into two five-note phrases. Here is the basic scoring of each repetition:

1. Pizzicato strings for both tune and refrain
2. Solo flute (tune); pizzicato strings (refrain)
3. Flute plus piccolo (tune); pizzicato strings (refrain)
4. Oboe followed by bassoon, phrase by phrase (tune); pizzicato strings (refrain), all accompanied by the Rhythm (slightly expanded: dum, dadadum, dum) on pizzicato cellos and basses—in addition to the continuous snare drum
5. Muted trumpet and two muted trombones (tune); pizzicato strings (refrain), accompanied by the Rhythm on low pizzicato strings and piano

Symphony No. 7

6. A canon (round) at one bar's distance, beginning on clarinet and E-flat clarinet, followed by oboe and English horn (tune); pizzicato strings (refrain); the Rhythm continues with a little harmonic enrichment from the piano
7. Violins (tune); full strings played normally (refrain); lower woodwinds join the Rhythm
8. Violins, violas, cellos, oboes, and clarinets (tune); strings, horns, and lower woodwinds (refrain); timpani and low brass join the Rhythm
9. Horns, low strings, and low woodwinds (tune); full strings, low woodwinds, trumpets, trombones, and tuba (refrain); the Rhythm moves to the violins, high woodwinds, and xylophone
10. Three trumpets and two trombones (tune); full strings, lower woodwinds, and lower brass (refrain), over which the horns blast out a related descending five-note phrase (the Descant); the Rhythm becomes a wailing accompaniment in strings and high woodwinds punctuated by crashes on the cymbals and bass drum; a second snare drum assists with the ongoing military rhythm
11. Violins and high woodwinds (tune); strings, full brass, and lower woodwinds (refrain), with the high woodwinds taking over the Descant; cymbals, bass drum, and tambourine take over the Rhythm while the rest of the orchestra produces a heaving, seasick accompaniment
12. Trumpets, trombones, and tuba (tune); same plus horns (refrain), with violins and high woodwinds getting the Descant; everyone else—with xylophone—plays a simple accompaniment in steady quarter notes, finally abandoning the Rhythm; the bass drum joins the two snare drums

This passage has been the subject of much misunderstanding, beginning with the frequent assertion that its main theme is new.

In fact, it derives almost entirely from elements of the first subject. The omnipresence of the Rhythm is one such element. Another is the fact that the actual tune consists of short phrases, every single one of which ends with two repeated notes, just like that exposed four-note woodwind phrase previously mentioned. Indeed, as the tune continues, its derivation from this original simple idea becomes increasingly evident, and the Descant is almost identical to it. Finally, the snare-drum motive itself is based on rapid groups of five notes, with which the first subject is liberally peppered. You can actually hear it stated almost completely in the rhythm of the strings in the symphony's tenth and eleventh bars, just before the woodwinds get the main theme for the first time.

So the reality is that there's very little new here at all. What Shostakovich has done is simply to take the most primitive, basic bits of his first subject and turn them into a trite, irritating little march that is incapable of doing anything except get louder. It's a perfect musical embodiment of the "bondage of the spirit" he mentioned. The opening theme's rhythmic, harmonic, and melodic elements are thus shackled and constrained, mindlessly mechanized, and rendered banal. Notice also that the tender second subject has nothing whatsoever to do with this process and indeed is entirely absent from the development section. It represents a haven of innocence and peace, about which more shortly, but the important point to understand is that the so-called Nazi march is not something alien, but rather a trivialized distortion of the first subject, a good idea that has given birth to a bad one.

Meanwhile, back in the development section, the Descant has tried to interpose itself at the end of the last few repetitions of the march tune. The twelfth and last of them isn't complete. Shostakovich's extra brass section (three each of trumpets and trombones) interrupts with a more fully developed version of the Descant in the guise of a new theme, simply accompanied by repeated chords backed by tambourine. This tune also has phrases ending in two repeated notes. A third snare drum now joins in, keeping up the omnipresent military rhythm. The march tune reacts with fury at the attempted digression, and Shostakovich unleashes an orchestral maelstrom as the two ideas battle it out for dominance, neither one coming out on top, possibly because there isn't really much difference between them. It's a clear case of mutually assured destruction; the music devours itself from within.

At the height of the commotion, after a huge crescendo ending with a sharp (and frequently insufficiently audible) whack on the tam-tam, the snare drums finally cut out, and at the top of a huge upward scale for the full orchestra, the recapitulation begins as a tragic outcry, still at top volume. The opening theme returns to crashes on tam-tam and cymbals, as well thunderous reiterations of the Rhythm on timpani and bass drum. It culminates at the point where Shostakovich first presented the descending four-note woodwind motive ending with two repeated notes, only now this takes the form of the Descant (that is, five notes), blasted out by the brass and topped by huge cymbal crashes. Or maybe this is a free inversion of the march theme (that is, the melody played upside down)? It doesn't matter, because as the music now makes pellucidly clear, it's the same idea either way.

As the shocking realization sinks in that the once-happy first subject was in fact the cause of all the ensuing mayhem, the nightmare recedes to the sound of gentler strains from the flute and violins. But the second subject, when it shortly arrives, offers a shock of a different kind. Instead of sweetness and lyricism, it has become a lament for solo bassoon over broken rhythms played by pizzicato lower strings and sharp chords on the piano. So this theme too, although not a participant in the chaotic development, has not avoided its devastating consequences.

The desolate recasting of the remainder of this recapitulation section necessitates a large coda, a summation of the musical argument. Two soft reiterations of the Rhythm from the horns reintroduce the first subject as at the symphony's opening. It swiftly gathers energy, reaching the woodwind climax with the descending four-note motive, now returned to its original form but breaking off midphrase. This motive may have had significance for Shostakovich beyond this symphony. It appears again at the central climax of the second movement of the Tenth Symphony, the famous "Stalin" scherzo.

Again the Rhythm, followed by an evanescent memory of the most tender bit of the second subject. The Rhythm interrupts one last time as the snare drum begins its militant tattoo once more, very softly, underpinned by isolated cymbal and bass drum strokes, as well as the broken accompaniment of the second subject's lament. A muted trumpet slyly recalls three phrases of the march tune, as percussion and piano cut the music off once and for all with a few dry chords. The forces of destruction can't be defeated, Shostakovich suggests, because we carry them within ourselves, and nothing is more calamitous than a banal idea that acquires the violent power to overwhelm all possible challenges to its supremacy. It may be, then, that Fascism cannot be described in abstract symphonic music, but the corrupting influence of an all-encompassing, spirit-crushing vulgarity can be.

Second Movement: Moderato (poco allegretto)

This perfectly proportioned movement, which comes across mainly as a calm, contrasting interlude between its far more imposing neighbors, has the shape ABACDCABA. It begins with one of those nonchalant, emotionally ambivalent string tunes characteristic of Shostakovich's slow scherzos. You will encounter another in the third movement of the Tenth Symphony. Second violins lead off, followed by the firsts, gradually settling down to a pulsating accompaniment that might owe something to the finale ("The Farewell") of Mahler's *Das Lied von der Erde*. Over this the B section begins with a sinuous melody from the solo oboe, then the English horn, and eventually the cellos, adding a brief gust of passion. This wends its way back to the opening string theme once again, even more thinly scored: just the tune with the lightest possible of accompaniments from pizzicato cellos and basses.

The central C episode erupts suddenly, in triple time and in a quicker tempo, with E-flat clarinet squealing a gawky melody that might have come from Prokofiev. The two composers seldom sound much alike, but there *are* moments. As the energy increases, xylophone and tambourine join in the fray, and with another sudden switch back to duple time, trumpets and violins announce a brilliant march theme (D). Its appearance is brief. The episode's initial tune returns, the texture becoming increasingly wild until a xylophone tremolo, like chattering teeth, precedes a final outburst that gradually evaporates, leaving the initial string melody (A), as at the beginning. Once again this leads to the slinky oboe tune, now darkened and mellowed by being given to the bass clarinet—a wonderful, hollow sound. The accompaniment is also transformed by a trio of flutes (including the alto member of the family) into a fluttering shadow of its former self. A brief clarinet solo serves as prelude to the last appearance of the movement's principal theme, which fades out, as it began, in the strings.

Third Movement: Adagio

This beautiful slow movement opens with one of Shostakovich's most arresting ideas: a chorale for harps and the entire woodwind section (except flutes) alternates with an impassioned violin recitative, making a gradual diminuendo on each repetition. The repetitions are not identical, so the general impression is of an ongoing dialogue having a stark, quasi-liturgical character. A similar process reappears in the slow movement of the Fifteenth Symphony as well. The length of this adagio, about eighteen minutes in most performances, is explained by the fact that, like the first movement, it is in strict sonata form, with a large development section. This entire initial complex of exchanges between strings and winds constitutes the first subject, and at such a slow tempo, each episode necessarily takes time.

A short pizzicato transition leads to the second subject. The strings continue their plucked accompaniment in two-note spurts, over which the flute sings a consoling melody in a sweet major key. The flute's solo soon becomes a duet. Because he's considered such a "heavy" composer, it's often overlooked that Shostakovich had a very special affection for the flute, whose light timbre dominates much of this symphony, as it also does the Fifth. Shostakovich, like Mozart, liked to color entire works with the timbre of particular woodwind instruments. In the Eighth Symphony, it's the English horn; in the Tenth, the clarinet. The violins continue the flute's theme in a lovely variation that leads without pause into the development section.

This begins with a return to the opening chorale, now on harps and strings, in combination with further variations of the violin melody just heard. The effect is sadly evocative, as the melody segues into a further repetition of the opening violin recitative, pianissimo. Suddenly the violins get a hold of a galloping rhythm, and like a shot, the music takes off with a vigorous variation of the second subject. The entry of the snare drum turns the tune into a bold march—Shostakovich marks this passage "resolutely," and that's just how it sounds. Like many of his movements in sonata form, including the first of this very symphony, the development section steadily increases in tension in order to spill over into a fortissimo recapitulation.

Listen for the cymbal crash, as over the rhythm of the strings and winds, the opening chorale returns on the full brass section, followed by a heroic statement of the initial string recitative on trumpets. After an even more impressive diminuendo-in-dialogue than previously, the same pizzicato transition brings back the second subject, now taking on a darker hue as a lengthy solo for the entire viola section. Once more the chorale returns softly on the strings, initiating the coda. This begins with the opening violin recitative, making its first full return since the beginning of the movement—recall that the recapitulation gave this tune to the trumpets. The strings interpose the chorale fortissimo, the violins answer, and the movement ends in darkness, with the chorale on clarinets, bass clarinet, and contrabassoon. Three soft strokes on the tam-tam provide the finishing touch.

Fourth Movement: Allegro non troppo

Softly rolling timpani link the adagio to the finale, a simple ABA structure in which the final return of A doubles as the coda. The transition to the quicker tempo is imperceptible, as bits of theme drift about in long notes in the strings. But the appearance of slowness is deceptive. There's really only one little motive that you need to look out for: a six-note leaping figure ominously uttered by the cellos and basses after the initial groping passage for violins. From this small idea, much of the important thematic material will grow, and for the next several minutes, just enjoy the gathering excitement and energy, as Shostakovich builds the music into a wild Cossack dance, very Russian in character.

The opening episode ends with a strikingly rhythmic violin melody accompanied by "snap" pizzicatos—plucked so hard that the string rebounds against the wood of the fingerboard. Mahler pioneered the effect in his own Seventh Symphony, and Bartók made it standard practice. The B section, in tempo moderato, develops a five-note idea that combines the rhythm of the initial phrases of the first movement's tacky march tune with the harmonies of the adagio's chorale. It neatly ties together the symphony's diverse range of materials. This idea also serves Shostakovich in another, very unexpected context: as the first prelude in his 24 Preludes and Fugues, Op. 87, for solo piano.

The remainder of the movement is coda, building itself up from the six-note leaping figure heard at the beginning of the movement. This appears mostly in timpani and brass, while horns, violins, and high woodwinds provide an accompaniment based on another familiar motive: the Rhythm. A big crescendo brings in the cymbals, and with them the symphony's opening theme in long notes on the trombones, triumphantly striding among the celebrating throng. As usual with Shostakovich in his heroic mode, the actual ending is hard won: the brass, backed by snare drums and then pounding timpani and bass drum, insist on the ominous leaping figure until the very last roof-raising chord.

Interestingly this finale, although even more overwhelmingly loud and (potentially) bombastic than that of the Fifth, has never had its sincerity of utterance questioned to the same degree. This may be because the symphony is so heavily front-loaded, and the first movement so controversial, that the ending isn't an issue. It's also perfectly apt as a conclusion to such a large work, far and away Shostakovich's longest symphony. In most performances it lasts around seventy-five minutes, and audiences are understandably grateful for the big payoff, having sat through such a lengthy and emotionally intense musical statement.

In fact, although it became wildly popular during the Second World War for obvious reasons and was equally widely derided for a long time thereafter, the "Leningrad" remains popular with conductors, orchestras, and audiences now used to big, late-romantic symphonies by composers such as Bruckner and Mahler. When played with conviction, it's a thrilling experience, but it can also be a monumental bore when delivered with anything less than total commitment. Like many Shostakovich works today, it's often played too slowly, with too little tempo contrast and dynamic range. The ending should leave your ears ringing and your neighbors complaining. For such an epic symphony, dealing with such major issues, nothing less will do.

Symphony No. 8
1943

Orchestration: 2 piccolos, 4 flutes, 2 oboes, English horn, E-flat clarinet, 2 clarinets, bass clarinet, 3 bassoons, contrabassoon, 3 trumpets, 4 horns, 3 trombones, tuba, timpani, triangle, snare drum, bass drum, 2 cymbals, tam-tam, xylophone, tambourine, strings

The Second World War paradoxically offered Soviet artists a breath of creative freedom. In the first place, the authorities obviously had things on their minds other than a strict enforcement of the tenets of Socialist Realism and, in any case, could count on a rare unanimity of legitimate artistic and patriotic sentiments. This produced, for example, Shostakovich's "Leningrad" Symphony, Prokofiev's Fifth, and other works in which a certain degree of musical populism doesn't dilute the quality of the composition as a whole. The war also afforded a pretext to write music of a much darker character than usual, with the avowed intent of commemorating the dead or expressing the suffering of the Russian people. The Eighth Symphony falls into this latter category.

A glance at the orchestration reveals a comparative austerity of means that would remain with Shostakovich until the cinematic Eleventh Symphony of 1957. There's no harp, piano, or celesta. After the huge forces required by the "Leningrad" Symphony of two years previously, the brass section is back to normal size, and the treatment of the woodwinds emphasizes the lower members of the family, with the plangent tones of the English horn especially prominent. This is also Shostakovich's first symphony in five parts (preceded in the chamber-music medium by the Piano Quintet of 1940) with the last three movements linked together, a format that will return in the Ninth and Thirteenth Symphonies as well. More importantly, this is the first Shostakovich symphony since the (as yet unheard) Fourth to dare to end quietly. It was a decision that would cost him dearly when the brief wartime period of relative artistic freedom came to an end, and a new round of denunciations—with this gut-wrenching symphony as a primary target—began in 1948.

First Movement: Adagio

From a structural point of view, this darkly imposing, twenty-five-minute-long movement in Shostakovich's favorite slow-tempo sonata form is a bigger, grimmer cousin to the first movement of the Fifth Symphony. Comparison of the opening string gestures reveals a melodic similarity as well, and like its predecessor, the piece is essentially monothematic. In other words, all its important ideas are present from the outset, in the first subject group, with new ideas derived from preceding ones. Indeed, this symphony is one of Shostakovich's most concentrated, with all five movements growing organically from the tiny three-note cell on cellos and basses with which the work begins. It is present throughout and plainly audible in all the principal melodic material, either in its initial "V" shape (that is, with the middle note lower than the two outer ones) or inverted, with the middle note higher: "Λ." In its initial form, this motive permeates the first two movements, while the inverted version dominates the last three.

After the opening exhortation, the first subject proceeds as in the Fifth Symphony, in a verse-and-refrain form whereby the opening gesture returns after each melodic climax. The atmosphere is bleaker, though, and the scoring is even more monochrome, more heavily weighted towards the string section. Even at this slow tempo, however, the music should move forward purposefully. For this reason, Shostakovich has taken pains to underline the violin's first tune with a pulsating accompaniment that has an important role to play in the development section. You can tell that the end of the first subject has arrived by the fact that the full wind section finally takes over to effect the necessary transition to the equally string-centered second subject, and also to create a welcome timbral contrast.

Once again, as in the Fifth, the tempo picks up for a more consoling second subject in ABA form. Over a gently urgent rhythmic accompaniment, the violins calmly sing out a theme that purports to be new but is in fact derived from the symphony's opening, with its note values greatly stretched out (or *augmented*). The central section consists of smoothly overlapping phrases based on rising scales, like a succession of sighs, with an expressive solo for English horn along the way, hesitantly leading back to a slightly varied return of the violin theme. All of these elements are very easy to describe and to hear, but because of the slow tempo, the music necessarily takes its time and requires patience from the listener. Everything about this movement is planned on a particularly large scale, including the development section, which is one of the most volcanic that Shostakovich ever wrote.

It begins with the opening motive intoned by a pair of flutes in their lowest register, a notably hollow and eerie sound, and continues in four distinct stages:

1. After the flutes, the theme gradually permeates the rest of the woodwind section, then the strings from the bottom up,

increasing in urgency and volume as it builds through the orchestra.
2. The beginning's pulsating accompaniment becomes an orchestral cudgel pounded out by timpani and low brass, followed by snare drum, while the violins restate their first theme with ever-increasing urgency. As the rhythmic energy increases, so does the hysteria, with wild woodwind runs and "snap" pizzicatos in the strings. A series of crescendos on suspended cymbal leads to a rending, dissonant climax, at the height of which:
3. The tempo increases to allegro non troppo (quick, but not too much so). Over jerky rhythms in the strings clearly deriving from the opening measures, woodwinds hurl out the actual tune in broken phrases. Remember this idea: it will serve as the basis for the third-movement toccata. Once again the tension accumulates, this time as the horn section panics in a series of very difficult unison passages in triplets, to which Shostakovich adds a clattering xylophone.
4. As the horn calls rise to a fever pitch, a grotesque march struts in, brutalizing the second subject in a series of staggered entries between the heavy brass on the one hand and woodwinds plus strings (with xylophone) on the other. The tempo is now a straight allegro and the mood one of utmost violence.

The moment of recapitulation is arguably the most cataclysmic that Shostakovich ever designed, and that's saying a lot. Over massive crescendos from timpani, bass drum, and snare drum, the opening motive returns on the full brass section, accented by cymbal crashes and woodwind trills. Trumpets complete the phrase, atop one last triple-forte wave of sound and a crash on the tam-tam. This leads not to the first-subject violin theme but to an extended English-horn lament—a very different procedure from that in the Fifth Symphony, where Shostakovich cuts directly to his second subject. Here, the English horn continues right past the point where the second subject begins (you can tell because its rhythmic accompaniment returns), and the recapitulation continues with its B section, followed at last by A in cellos and basses.

The coda features one last return of the opening motive, more malevolent than ever on sneering muted trumpets and horns. There's also good reason for Shostakovich's decision to withhold the violin tune from the first subject in favor of that English horn solo. He saves it for use here, where it now appears in those instruments in a free inversion (that is, played upside down), resigned and tranquil. In this atmosphere of uneasy calm, with just a touch of trumpet tone reserved for the very end, the music slowly fades out of hearing, one of Shostakovich's longest and most emotionally draining first movements.

Second Movement: Allegretto

The relationship between the first and second movements of this symphony recalls that of Mahler's Sixth, in that the second is a parody of the first, sharing several important elements. The opening on lower strings, for example, clearly recalls the motive that opens the work, and the squealing woodwinds, with their three-note figures, bring to mind the similar episode in the previous movement's development section. It's important to recognize, however, that in unifying the piece this way, Shostakovich is not being repetitious. These simple motives are always modified, recombined, rescored, and constantly evolving. There's a world of difference between the earnestness of the first movement and the clunky grotesquerie on display here.

Like its predecessor, this movement is in sonata form, and the second subject is related to the first even though it is in 3/4 time as opposed to the opening's 4/4 march tempo. Cast mainly as a very lightly accompanied solo for piccolo, assisted now and then by other members of the woodwind family, the element in common is a quick descending scale of four or five notes, often at the ends of phrases, that gives the music a slippery quality, like a mountaineer skidding down a steep slope. The very brief development section consists largely of a jumbled dialogue between woodwinds (mostly) and strings (a bit later), all based on this common element, plus the symphony's three-note motto. This gradually traces the shape and sound of the actual theme with which the movement began.

The moment of recapitulation is particularly easy to hear: Shostakovich has reserved the full percussion section, including tambourine, just for this point. As it comes crashing in, the music acquires an additional sense of menace that's hard not to compare to the percussion-led recap of the previous movement. The first subject is louder now but also shorter in length, as the second interrupts with its rhythmic accompaniment on jarring low brass and bass drum, urged on by a persistent snare drum. The coda returns to march tempo and the principal theme, in a long-drawn diminuendo punctuated by snare drum and xylophone, leading to what appears to be a quiet close. But with a sudden crescendo from brass and percussion, solo timpani bang the door shut with the symphony's three-note motto.

Third Movement: Allegro non troppo

This movement is a toccata, quite similar in style to the episode so described in the finale of the Fourth Symphony. What this means in practice is a piece in perpetual motion. Accordingly, maintaining the rhythm is Shostakovich's primary concern, and while knowledge of the previous example gives some sense of what kind of music this is, its emotional effect in context couldn't be more different. In the Fourth Symphony, the effect of the toccata is one of unaffected brilliance, while here it conveys inhuman savagery. Shostakovich achieves this in a manner similar to the technique used in creating the march episode in the first movement of the Seventh Symphony: by taking a couple of primitive elements common to previous themes (and in this case, the symphony as a whole) and repeating them mechanically over and over, with ever-increasing power and menace.

This particular toccata has a simple ABA form. Its opening section consists of a monotonous rhythm that becomes a sort of rudimentary theme based on the inverted (Λ) shape of the symphony's motto. Over this idea, announced by the violas, the woodwinds—piercing E-flat clarinet in particular—do what they do best: shrilly scream out a similarly simplified version of the motto. Violins take over from the violas, and Shostakovich adds a new sound effect: jarring thuds consisting of timpani riffs, short blasts from trombones and tuba, and "snap" pizzicatos in the lower strings. Another series of woodwind cries passes the toccata theme to the trombones (a seriously virtuoso passage), with the trumpets taking over the woodwind part. Next, the orchestra breaks up the toccata rhythm into two-note fragments, the pizzicato strings alternating with woodwinds and horns. A seesawing passage for the full string section with off-beat brass leads back to the most heavily scored version of the toccata's theme-plus-screech complex yet, leaving the cellos and basses to execute an impressive diminuendo while keeping up the steady rhythm all the while.

The B section is a dashing, militant trumpet solo, also based on the toccata theme, interspersed with snare-drum solos and commentary from the violins and high woodwinds, all accompanied by a steady "oompah" rhythm from quiet trombones, tuba, bass drum, and cymbals. The mood, if not exactly cheerful, is certainly more upbeat—with a brash, macho quality—but it quickly yields to a return of the toccata, bizarrely rescored for violins (with downward glissandos), xylophone, and muted trombones. This repeat is substantially shortened, moving quickly through the next two sections, until solo covered (to dull the sound) timpani get the main theme, and the full brass section screams in panic. This juggernaut of terror swiftly reaches an apocalyptic climax as snare drum, two cymbal players, bass drum, and tamtam deliver three crushing fusillades, the last of which blows the movement to smithereens. Technically, this concluding paroxysm of violence belongs to the . . .

Fourth Movement: Largo

. . . which follows without pause. This is a passacaglia, a form that, like the toccata, has its origins in the baroque period. You can find passacaglias not just in this symphony but also in the First Violin Concerto, Fifteenth Symphony, Second Piano Trio, and Tenth Quartet, always as slow movements. The whole point of this type of piece, at least as used by Shostakovich, is its solemnity, an effect produced by the constantly repeating bass line (which is the basic definition of a passacaglia), over which various instruments meditate introspectively. This particular example features twelve full statements by the cellos and basses (assisted by the brass the first time through) of its main idea, which unusually has an irregular length of nine bars. The theme is also very clearly related both melodically and rhythmically to the principal violin tune in the first movement's first subject.

One expressive effect of the irregular bar length of the bass is that the music above it, which adopts different phrasing, is not cleanly synchronized with each repetition. The resulting rhythmic independence detaches the melody from its accompaniment and allows it to float, rootless, giving the movement a numb, drifting quality, representing a devastatingly logical reaction to the preceding brutality. In short, this is music in a state of shock. After the brass and strings announce what will become the subject of the passacaglia, a dazed threnody builds up in the order: second violins, violas, first violins. This covers cycles 2–5 of the bass theme. Next comes a wistful horn solo that lasts a bit longer than the sixth recurrence, after which (atop No. 7) piccolo and flute warble like lost birds in a desolate landscape (recall the similar image in the opening movement of the Sixth Symphony).

This yields to a remarkable passage (repeat No. 8) for pizzicato strings and a quartet of flutter-tonguing flutes, a particularly ghostly sound. Once this subsides, a solo clarinet takes over the stylized birdsong (repeat No. 9). As this slowly morphs into a gentle, syncopated rhythmic pulsation, the first violins intone the passacaglia theme in close canon with the cellos and basses—that is, as if they were playing a round—completing its tenth circuit. The eleventh brings back the clarinet arabesques one last time, along with a soft comment from the violins, and finally, at the twelfth appearance of the theme, Shostakovich offers a touch more flutter-tonguing from the flutes. Two clarinets plus bass clarinet have the last word over fading cellos and basses, linking this movement to the finale with a hopeful, hesitant modulation to a major key.

One word of caution: this entire movement takes place, after its traumatic beginning, at a very low dynamic level. It has no climaxes; aside from the initial outburst and that single timid horn, no brass instruments take part and no percussion. Of the woodwinds, only flutes and clarinets play, and they are the softest, most mellow members of their section as well. Don't expect big contrasts, and above all don't worry about counting each appearance of the passacaglia theme. The effect of the music is intentionally timeless and hypnotic; just lose yourself in it for ten to twelve minutes.

Fifth Movement: Allegretto

This marvelous finale, always acclaimed as one of Shostakovich's finest, neatly sums up the entire musical content of the symphony in a way that's also particularly emotionally apt. It represents a return to life after the stunned silence of the passacaglia, but one in which the happiness is forced and hollow. If this symphony were about a "hero" in the typical romantic sense, you might say that he survives, seriously wounded. The music walks with a limp. In terms of form, this movement is equally wonderful, a combination of sonata and rondo that sounds like this: ABAC–development [fugue]–ADCA. It's put together with absolutely Mozartian finesse and scored, for the most part, with real delicacy, exuding an innocent sweetness that's all the more heartbreaking as a result.

Two bassoons plus contrabassoon lead off, with a ritornello theme permeated by the symphony's three-note motto. The violins answer with a sighing variation, very similar to their music at the end of the second movement. Shostakovich often writes chromatic, gliding melodies like this one, and they always seem to express a sort of resignation or exhaustion. Flute and triangle suggest happier thoughts and launch the B episode, which includes a more serious melody for cellos. This leads back to the ritornello, now on oboes and English horn, and brought to the most positive climax yet as developed and extended by the strings. In the next section (C), bassoons, bass clarinet, and cellos play a queasy, comical tune against quacking trombones, full of chromatic scales and digressions. The violins also participate, interjecting caustic repetitions of the three-note motto.

What sounds like a return of A on soft cellos and basses turns out to be an expansive fugal development, in which each group of strings enters one after the other, then the woodwinds do the same (in the order: flute, English horn, bassoon, clarinet, with an additional part in free counterpoint from the oboe along the way). Like most instrumental fugues, this one has the character of a discussion or argument, over the course of which Shostakovich gradually reassembles the orchestra section by section, leading to the robust recapitulation. Here the ritornello appears for the first time in the trumpets, horns, and trombones, with isolated timpani shots in between its phrases. The music remains bold and confident as the tempo increases to allegro, and a new motive in cellos and basses recalls the rhythm of the symphony's opening gesture. This turns out to be prophetic: the atmosphere darkens, and with startling abruptness, the climax of the first movement returns (D), with its crushing drum rolls and cymbal crashes, in a grindingly dissonant variation.

Heavy brass and pounding timpani take over and briefly extend the terror beyond its previous shape, resolving at last in a huge "amen" from the entire orchestra. This nightmare vision effectively sucks the wind out of the movement. Episode C now resumes on solo bass clarinet and solo violin, its cheer sounding tragically empty. A trio of bassoons—followed by violins, just like the movement's beginning—then offers a final gentle reminder of the ritornello, as the music comes to rest on a long-held chord in the strings. Against this, a few pizzicatos and a low tone from the flute outline the three-note motto, with quizzical gestures in between. Shostakovich repeats this pianissimo "question and answer" formula long enough to suggest an infinite horizon, stretching out past the point where the music actually stops.

Symphony No. 9
1945

Orchestration: piccolo, 2 flutes, 2 oboes, 2 clarinets, 2 bassoons, 2 trumpets, 4 horns, 3 trombones, tuba, timpani, triangle, snare drum, bass drum, cymbals, tambourine, strings

If anyone ever seriously questions Shostakovich's fundamental artistic independence and courage, just point to this symphony. It caused him a world of trouble. Like the Eighth, it has five movements, the last three of which are linked together, but the resemblance ends there. The entire work lasts about as long as its predecessor's first movement alone—twenty-five minutes or so on average—and in terms of both form and expression, it's strictly neoclassical, paying obvious homage to the tradition of Haydn and Mozart. Does that make it a work strictly for connoisseurs? Not at all. It remains one of Shostakovich's most approachable, popular, and frequently played works. The orchestration—with its reduced ensemble requirements, sparing use of percussion, and lack of low-pitched woodwind extras such as English horn, bass clarinet, and contrabassoon—gives some idea of the work's comparatively bright, even comic, character.

So why did this symphony cause Shostakovich so much trouble? Simple. Communist authorities are not known for their sense of humor. They expected a grand choral work to celebrate

Russia's heroic sacrifice and victory in World War II, and what they got instead was a comedy act. Humor in music has always been undervalued and misunderstood, whether the composer was Haydn (who basically invented it), Mahler, or anyone else, but nowhere was it less appreciated than in Soviet Russia in 1945. It was a case of bad timing. Shostakovich really did have a wicked sense of humor, and his failure to perform as expected in this work, combined with the gloomy Eighth, led directly to a new round of official denunciations in 1948.

The symphony's fastidiousness and clarity also reveal Shostakovich's increasing involvement throughout the 1940s with chamber music and, in particular, with his cycle of fifteen string quartets, which really got going during this period. The Third Quartet, written in 1946, also adopts a five-movement shape, and there's an even more fascinating formal correspondence between the Eighth and Ninth Symphonies and the Eighth and Ninth Quartets (1960 and 1964, respectively). All four pieces require five movements, and moreover, these largely correspond in tempo and character (with minor differences in internal order) between the similarly numbered works. In addition, both of the "8s" are in C minor, and both "9s" in E-flat major, sharing remarkably consistent expressive qualities as well. Somehow I doubt that this was accidental, but what it means—if anything—is an open question.

First Movement: Allegro

Odd as it may seem, this is the first traditional sonata-allegro opening movement in a Shostakovich symphony. What this means is that the quick tempo is maintained throughout, for both first and second subjects. There's even an exposition repeat, just like in Haydn and Mozart, and none of Shostakovich's other works in this genre has that distinction. A spirit of good-humored, child-like banter rules here. Violins begin quietly with a phrase that's a faster relative of the one that opens the second movement of Seventh Symphony, followed by flute, violins again, then oboe. The tunes are catchy, short, and simple in character, and each instrument has its own distinct melodic personality. Pay special attention to the shape of that rising oboe phrase: it will become, in simplified form, the principal theme of the finale.

The second subject is a march, introduced by solo trombone and snare drum. Its tune, whistled by the solo piccolo backed by triangle, is as carefree and charming as Shostakovich knows how to be. You get to hear it twice, barked out by trumpets and trombones the second time through, but only mezzo forte and without a shred of militancy. A couple of up-and-down exchanges between strings and winds bring the exposition to close, and then it's back to the beginning once again. The boisterous development section takes both subjects in order. It only lasts a minute or two, and just as the march tune sounds as if it's growing hostile, a loud thwack on the bass drum (its only appearance in the entire symphony) sends the brass section careening off course and into the very funny recapitulation, which continues at the same loud volume.

The orchestra now goes right on developing the first subject, despite the trombone's ongoing attempts to introduce the second. After several vain and increasingly desperate efforts, the rest of the orchestra takes notice of what it's supposed to be doing, and the march returns as a winsome violin solo. The coda indulges in a bit more development, including a return to the more militant version of the second subject, before the rest of the orchestra shrugs the whole thing off with a series of trills and a firm final cadence. It's a delightful, breezy movement that, like the classical masters it emulates, strikes a perfect balance between tart and sweet.

Second Movement: Moderato

This slowish movement—a simple ABABA—in keeping with classical-period precedent omits the trumpets, heavy brass, timpani, and percussion. That means that the scoring for woodwinds is particularly sensitive. The music has a lonely, nostalgic quality that's very memorable but quite far from the benumbed terror characteristic of some of Shostakovich's larger works. A solo clarinet has the opening melody, accompanied lightly by pizzicato cellos and basses. The solo becomes a duet, grows to encompass the entire wind section, and then diminishes once again to end as it began.

Shifting time signatures prevent the opening tune from establishing a clear rhythm, but the B section, for strings, is a hesitant waltz with sighing chromatics that approaches and recedes several times before A returns as a flute solo. Once again the waltz intervenes on the strings, then the opening appears for the last time on flute and clarinets, followed by a coda in adagio tempo featuring solo piccolo. The form may be incredibly simple, but the melodies stand among Shostakovich's finest. He's seldom given credit for being a tunesmith, but this movement demonstrates that when everything depends on the quality of the themes, he doesn't disappoint.

Third Movement: Presto

This tiny scherzo, a chipper piece close in mood to the second movement of the Sixth Symphony, is in 6/8 time, unusual for Shostakovich. He treats this rhythm for the most part as two beats per measure, with three notes to each beat. Woodwinds cavort about at high speed, with a theme possibly derived from the first movement's opening melody. The accompanying rhythms in the strings are very characteristic of Spanish folk music—no castanets here, but use your imagination—particularly when it comes to the central episode. This dashing trumpet theme might recall the similar instrumental solo at the center of the Eighth Symphony's third-movement toccata, but the tune here has more bravado than ferocity, and it runs directly into a return of the opening at top speed. The repeat proceeds normally at first, then the orchestration starts to thin out bit by bit, the tempo slows down, and before you know it, the movement glides to a halt. It has lasted a bit less than three minutes.

Fourth Movement: Largo

This largo, which serves as a bridge between the scherzo and the finale, gives the lower brass—otherwise used with exceptional discretion—a brief moment to shine. Its form is schematically simple: ABAB. The A section is simply a stentorian proclamation from the brass, capped by a crash on suspended cymbal, while B is an expressive recitative for solo bassoon. The alternation of the two produces an effect akin to the slow movement of Beethoven's Fourth Piano Concerto, where the piano acts as a calming influence after the aggressive statements of the strings. This movement is shorter and less highly developed, but the concept is a bit similar.

Fifth Movement: Allegretto

Having tamed the brass section, the solo bassoon also launches the finale with a simple "up and down" scale theme derived, as previously suggested, from the oboe phrase in the opening movement's first subject. This idea takes a few repetitions from strings and woodwinds in alternation to settle down and make up its mind what key it properly belongs in. The second subject, initially for violins alone, is a march—just like the corresponding theme in the first movement. Both tunes begin with three repeated notes, making their relationship especially clear, but the actual melody is quite close to the marchlike first subject that leads off the First Symphony.

The development section is one big crescendo based mainly on the movement's first subject, with just a touch of the second in the form of three repeated notes tripping up the rhythm. This builds up through the orchestra, layer by layer, until the full orchestra with tambourine bursts in with the recapitulation. Both main tunes pass by in highly compressed form as a single idea, with no transitional material at all. Suddenly the tempo increases to allegro, and the music races off in a breezy coda full of rhythmic high jinks, based on the scales of the first theme. It's a final indication of Shostakovich's finesse that this is the only time in the entire symphony that plate cymbals are used, and only at a soft dynamic level to mark the rhythm along with the triangle.

Violin Concerto No. 1
1947–48, revised 1955

Orchestration: solo violin, piccolo, 3 flutes, 3 oboes, English horn, 3 clarinets, bass clarinet, 3 bassoons, contrabassoon, 4 horns, tuba, timpani, xylophone, tam-tam, tambourine, 2 harps, celesta, strings

The First Violin Concerto is in many ways a stunning achievement. Its structure is unique in the orchestral works: a suite consisting of a mixture of baroque/classical formal types as well as romantic "character" pieces—specifically: a nocturne, a scherzo, a passacaglia, and a burlesque. Shostakovich first tried out this kind of arrangement in chamber music as early as 1940 in his Piano Quintet (billed as a prelude, fugue, scherzo, intermezzo, and finale) and followed up the discoveries made in that work with the Second String Quartet of 1944, which consists of an overture, a recitative and romance, a waltz, and a theme and variations. Both the Eleventh and Fifteenth Quartets (1966, 1974) also adopt the suite format, each having a different selection of movements.

Two symphonies, the Fourth and Eighth, also include some elements of suite-type construction—toccata, passacaglia, waltz, burlesque—but the First Violin Concerto is his only orchestral work to adopt this procedure exclusively and to designate its movements accordingly. It is thus the only concerto by Shostakovich without an opening movement in some version of sonata form, but it's no less weighty for that. Indeed, the range of expression here is unusually wide, and this, combined with its wealth of color, makes it one of a tiny handful of truly great violin concertos, right up there with those by Beethoven, Brahms, Sibelius, Mendelssohn, Tchaikovsky, and perhaps one or two others. Virtually all modern violin virtuosos include this work in their repertoire as a matter of course, beginning with its dedicatee, the legendary David Oistrakh, who recorded it several times.

Although the official dates of composition speak of a 1955 revision, the fact is that Shostakovich wrote the work in 1948 and then simply let it sit in his desk drawer. Other than small adjustments in rehearsal, he never altered a work significantly once it had been completed. The later date reflects the point at which he felt safe enough to unveil the work and allow a premiere. After the artistic purges of 1948, where he was once again singled out for abuse, he didn't dare release it for performance, and virtually all of his serious pieces written between 1948 and Stalin's death in 1953 fall into the category of works shelved for the future (see the chronological list of titles in appendix 1 for details).

By the time Oistrakh was finally able to play the new concerto, the artistic climate had changed considerably. Shostakovich was unquestionably the most famous living Russian composer, and although still subject to sniping and complaints from jealous colleagues in the Composer's Union, he had become a cultural commodity. At home he was routinely required to publish demeaning apologies for the "mistakes" contained in his latest works, while at the same time, his international acclaim continued to grow. Shostakovich's music—as played by a new generation of Soviet-trained virtuosos, including such legendary names as Oistrakh, Richter (piano), and Rostropovich (cello)—became a useful Cold War propaganda tool evidencing Russian artistic preeminence.

Distasteful as this confluence of culture and politics undoubtedly was, when it came to the First Violin Concerto, the authorities unwittingly had a point. It is without doubt a milestone in twentieth-century music.

First Movement: Nocturne (Moderato)

This is the only movement in the concerto to require the harps, celesta, and tam-tam, giving some indication of the music's darkly exotic, fantastic atmosphere. There is no firm sense of tonality: the harmony is restlessly chromatic and unstable, but both the opening melody on cellos and basses and the violin's lyrical answer contain recognizable motivic and rhythmic elements that are easy to hear whenever they return. Formally, the movement might be described as an improvisational series of seamlessly fluid variations on these initial ideas, but as its entire point is to create about twelve minutes of pure atmosphere, suffice it to say that when Shostakovich wants you to notice an important melodic element, you will. Otherwise, it doesn't matter a bit.

The scoring, aside from the instruments already mentioned, is notable for the fact that Shostakovich emphasizes the low members of the woodwind family: bass clarinet, bassoons, and contrabassoon. In fact, the three oboes play only a half-dozen bars at the movement's muted climax (it barely reaches forte), and this gives the accompaniments a rich, velvety texture over which the soloist sings what sounds like an endlessly searching melody. Shostakovich also withholds his "special effect" tone colors until nearly halfway through the movement, and they gain in prominence as the music proceeds, until at the very end, all that is left are the harps, celesta, and a soft tap on the tam-tam.

Second Movement: Scherzo (Allegro)

The opening theme of this scherzo, greatly slowed down, closely resembles that of the Tenth Symphony's third movement, but at this speed, with its constantly shifting meters and the solo interjecting sharp accents in odd places, it might at first strike you as a confused hubbub of chattering winds and frantic violin. This, of course, is Shostakovich's intention, for as the music proceeds, it starts to sort out the rhythm and assemble ideas of greater stability and breadth. In terms of form, this is a classical sonata-allegro, with a substantially recomposed recapitulation. Actually, the whole thing never stops developing from the moment flute and bass clarinet lead off in the very first bar, although once you know the music, it's quite easy to follow.

There are several important musical firsts in this dynamo of a movement, starting with the presence of Shostakovich's musical acronym, formed from the first letter of his first name (D) and the first three letters in the German spelling of his last (SCH). This produces the four-note motive: D, E-flat, C, B*. You can hear this motive in many works of this and later periods, including the Second Piano Trio, Second Piano Sonata, Tenth Symphony, Fifteenth Symphony, and Eighth Quartet. It appears in this movement for the first time, played loudly by the soloist about ninety seconds in, right after a grotesque passage for the full woodwind section (with ribald horn snorts) over bouncing two-note figures in the violin.

The next "first" arrives with the tambourine (used in this movement only) and xylophone, in the form of the second subject. This is a duple-meter dance of markedly Jewish cast, one of many such tunes that will pepper Shostakovich's music from

---

* In German usage, the note E-flat is pronounced "ess," like the letter S, and the letter B stands for the musical note B-flat, while H represents B-natural. Hence, DSCH = D, E-flat, C, B-natural.

this point onwards. His fascination and personal identification with Jewish melodies, which he described as expressing forced happiness, or "dancing through tears," also characterizes the Second Piano Trio and Fourth String Quartet, not to mention the song cycle *From Jewish Folk Poetry*. It will reach a sort of apotheosis in the Thirteenth Symphony, "Babi Yar," with its passionate denunciation of anti-Semitism. This particular example perfectly captures the brittle edge of desperation and bitterness behind its facade of good cheer.

On the other side of the Jewish episode, the solo violin returns to the initial themes in an extended developmental dialogue with various members of the woodwind section, making brief reference in passing to the second subject as well but staying in the opening triple meter. The formal recapitulation begins shortly thereafter on clarinet and bass clarinet, recalling the instrumental timbres at the movement's start, before a climactic statement of the main theme in the full orchestra leads to a ferocious duel between solo and ensemble that cuts directly back to the dance. Now the violin leads the celebration, with a thrumming pizzicato accompaniment providing rhythmic impetus. The second subject's return is short lived, however, as the music switches back to triple time, and with the soloist fiddling at full tilt, the music rushes to a surprisingly jovial major-key conclusion.

Third Movement: Passacaglia (Andante)

This movement, the heart of the work, achieves a passion and nobility of spirit virtually unequalled in the violin-concerto literature. As noted in the discussion of the Eighth Symphony, a passacaglia is basically a set of variations over a constantly repeated tune in the bass—although the principal subject may, and in this case will, migrate elsewhere over the course of the movement. The construction of this piece is absolutely wonderful, and so beautifully judged both formally and expressively that it cries out to be discussed in detail, if only for the sheer joy of describing it.

There are nine repetitions of the passacaglia theme, which very unusually has seventeen bars. As in the Eighth Symphony, the odd phrase-length helps to minimize the inherent rhythmic squareness of the form. In this piece, however, aside from the lyrical freedom given the soloist to glide across the bar lines, the musical surface tends to align more precisely with each repetition of the bass theme than Shostakovich finds desirable in the symphony. Here is an outline of each variation:

1. Cellos and basses announce the passacaglia theme, which incidentally is very similar in character to the one in the finale of the Fifteenth Symphony. Over this melody, mostly in four- or five-note phrases broken by rests, the horns intone a solemn fanfare, with timpani reinforcing first one part, then the other.
2. Tuba and third bassoon have the theme, over which English horn, clarinets, and the two remaining bassoons play a chorale of markedly liturgical character. Their sonority recalls that of an organ.
3. Cellos and basses have the theme, violas and violins play the woodwind chorale, and the solo violin now enters with a moving new melody on top of it all.
4. With the theme and chorale as before, English horn and bassoons play the previous violin melody, while the solo continues seamlessly with a further, more elaborately lyrical idea.
5. Horns, first solo, then two in unison, have the theme. The chorale remains in the upper strings, later joined by the woodwinds. Cellos and basses repeat the violin tune of the

fourth variation, while simultaneously the soloist moves on with increasing passion.
6. The theme moves to horns, tuba, and pizzicato cellos and basses. The woodwinds drop out, but the violas and violins keep on with the chorale. The solo plays an ever more urgent melody in triplet rhythm, recalling the opening horn fanfares. This entire variation is essentially a preparatory buildup to the next one.
7. The movement's climax: it has a remarkable emotional impact, even though (or because) it's scored only for strings. Violins and violas keep the chorale. Cellos and basses play a melodic counterpoint below, and the solo violin gets the passacaglia theme, fortissimo. It has the effect of a bright sunbeam bursting through a cloud-strewn sky.
8. This is a subdued recapitulation of variation No. 3, rescored. Tuba and bassoon have the theme, three clarinets the chorale, while the soloist plays the melody of its first entrance in a lower register.
9. The opening returns in a skeletal variation at the lowest possible dynamic level: timpani and pizzicato strings have the theme, while the soloist repeats the initial horn fanfares, the phrases increasingly fragmented.

A brief coda alternates bits of fanfare and passacaglia theme, as over a soft timpani roll and a long-held note in the cellos and basses, the soloist ascends, gently fading away to silence. Not least of this movement's orchestral wonders is the fact that Shostakovich completely omits the piccolo and flutes, creating a sonic tapestry of remarkable warmth despite the restrained scoring. This, combined with the prevalence of consonant, diatonic harmony, places the music about as far from the phantasmagorical, shimmering darkness of the first movement as it's possible to be while remaining within the same work.

Technically the solo cadenza that follows remains part of the Passacaglia, but in appendix 2, where I detail the formal layout of the symphonies and concertos, I list it as a separate movement, as Shostakovich himself does with the cadenza of the First Cello Concerto. At about five minutes in length (as long as the finale, in fact), it merits separate billing. Beginning with the Passacaglia's horn fanfares, it reviews much of the thematic material heard so far, including the DSCH motive and the Jewish dance from the Scherzo. As the tempo accelerates, the writing becomes increasingly wild, until with a series of eruptive glissandos, the finale bursts in without pause.

Fourth Movement: Burlesque (Allegro con brio)

When Shostakovich says "burlesque," he's not kidding. You may feel, on hearing the xylophone and woodwinds play the zany opening tune of this rondo, that you've heard it before. Indeed you have: it's the solo's main theme from the Nocturne, speeded up and adjusted harmonically to emphasize its goofiness, but with all its rhythmic and motivic elements firmly in place. After its initial appearance on the full orchestra, the violin takes over all the repeats of the rondo theme (or ritornello)*, while in the intervening episodes, the soloist cavorts about with the orchestra and introduces several new ideas. These include a galloping tune

---

* Incidentally, the opening of the finale is one point at which Shostakovich made changes to the 1948 score. He did it at the request of David Oistrakh. Originally, the violin had the rondo theme at the start of the movement, as it does on all subsequent occasions, but Oistrakh pointed out quite reasonably that after the emotional and physical strain of the Passacaglia and cadenza, it was cruel to ask the soloist to launch the finale and play another five minutes of very difficult music at top speed. He begged Shostakovich to give him a few measures "to wipe the sweat off my brow," and the composer agreed immediately, rescoring the opening of the finale for full orchestra instead.

featuring four repeated notes over an offbeat pizzicato accompaniment, and a descending melody in fast two-note phrases in dialogue between woodwinds in strings that somehow sounds very Russian and carnival-like.

At one point this latter tune morphs into what will become the main theme of the finale of the First Cello Concerto. There's also a particularly memorable parody of the Passacaglia, played in close overlap between high woodwinds and xylophone on the one hand and solo horn on the other. For the coda, the tempo increases to presto, as Shostakovich hurls out one bizarre motive after the next with maximum force, including a final bit of Passacaglia blasted out on the horns. The soloist continues fiddling away like mad in the highest register of the violin until the music comes blazing, full bore, to a sudden but emphatic close.

It's probably fair to consider the First Violin Concerto as the seminal Shostakovich work of the 1940s. It embodies so many musical elements that summarize his achievement to date and also point the way forward. These include its mixture of seriousness and humor, the use of the DSCH motive, the selection of baroque movement-types and its overall suite form, and the incorporation of Jewish dance elements. What makes the piece even greater is the fact that it's not just a fabulous vehicle for a virtuoso violinist, but it achieves its expressive intensity in terms of the composer's wholly personal idiom. In other words, this is a work of Shostakovich first and a violin concerto second, and the miracle is that there is no conflict at all between the two.

Symphony No. 10
1953

Orchestration: 2 piccolos, 2 flutes, 3 oboes, English horn, E-flat clarinet, 3 clarinets, 3 bassoons, contrabassoon, 3 trumpets, 4 horns, 3 trombones, tuba, timpani, triangle, snare drum, bass drum, cymbals, tambourine, tam-tam, xylophone, strings

On March 5, 1953, Josef Stalin died, an event that may have had an impact on the Tenth Symphony, composed between August and October of that same year. It is generally accepted that Shostakovich was being truthful in his description of the second movement as a "portrait of Stalin" (in the sense of evil run amok), and as you will see, this has very interesting consequences in considering the meaning of the happy finale. Of course, it's also possible that in this, his first symphony written and performed after the purges of 1948, Shostakovich dared not end tragically, as the last movement initially seems to want to, but no one has ever seriously questioned either the emotional sincerity or musical aptness of this particular conclusion. Indeed, the general consensus acclaims the Tenth as Shostakovich's finest symphony.

Like the First Violin Concerto, this piece has a confident mastery about it that tends to silence criticism. Its colorful orchestral language and surface excitement are matched by an intellectual depth that gives the music staying power well beyond the initial thrills of a first or second encounter. While arguably true of most of Shostakovich's more important works, it's a quality particularly easily grasped in this particular case, because he has taken care to make the large-scale form both within and between movements especially clear. In the Fourth Symphony, for example, part of the impact of the music's coruscating and garish exterior stems from its ability to present a simple basic structural idea as a bewildering collage of seemingly unrelated events. Here, however, Shostakovich builds on his experience in writing the Ninth, with its pellucid classical design, and combines exceptional formal clarity with an expressive range and impact more characteristic of the heroic Fifth, Seventh, or Eighth Symphonies. The result is incredibly moving and powerful, even for him.

Moderato

The opening is another of Shostakovich's slow sonata-form structures, similar in design to those in the Fifth and Eighth Symphonies, and accordingly characterized by the extreme tension that builds through the development section, culminating in an explosive return to the initial themes when the recapitulation begins. But there's also a big difference: this entire movement plays in a single basic moderato tempo, with only a few minor adjustments along the way for expressive purposes. All of Shostakovich's previous examples of this formal type increase in speed as they progress, reaching a genuine allegro in their central developments before returning in elegiac codas to the slower, darker music with which they began. And unlike the Tenth Symphony, his earlier efforts were largely monothematic, with all of the movement's principal melodic material clearly derived from a single common idea announced at the outset.

In this first movement, however, Shostakovich presents his musical argument without extreme changes of speed, although with clearly contrasted first and second subjects. The unusually rich melodic content is organized and developed in what are arguably the most cogently shaped musical paragraphs in any of these symphonies. The passage that begins the development and continues right up through the recapitulation of the second subject strikes the listener as a single, unified thought, perfectly proportioned and inexorable in its grandeur and forward drive. Under these circumstances, choosing the correct tempo in performance is critical, although many conductors ignore Shostakovich's "moderato" indication and play the music too slowly. On average, this movement should last about twenty-two minutes, with a maximum of approximately twenty-five. Any slower and it risks falling apart.

When listening to this symphony, pay special attention to the horns, which lead the brass section, and also the clarinets, whose mellow timbre tends to dominate the woodwinds. Another useful tip: focus on what's happening in the lower regions of the orchestra. Like the Eighth Symphony, this work has a "motto," here taking the form of the first six, ominous notes on the cellos and basses with which the first movement begins. These are divided into two rising phrases of three notes each, and this motive tends to remain in the bass register, with only a few exceptions. The music continues with a solemn passage for strings that, although darkly colored, has none of the anguish of the outwardly similar openings of the Fifth and Eighth Symphonies. It moves purposefully forward like a majestic river flowing through a shadowy landscape.

After the opening paragraph for strings alone (beneath which the motto comes and goes), the first subject continues with an elegiac theme for solo clarinet. Other instruments gradually join in as the music proceeds, moving inexorably to a powerful climax at whose summit the horns turn the motto upside down—just listen for its three-note phrases descending instead of ascending. You can't miss it. A short chorale for horns, trombones, and tuba leads to a modified reprise of the clarinet tune, which acts as a transition to the slightly faster second subject: a limping waltz for flute, then violins, over pizzicato strings. Notice how Shostakovich has avoided emphasizing the movement's basic triple time throughout the first subject, so that its dancelike quality only breaks through for the first time, however hesitantly, at this point.

In contrast to the opening themes, which are mostly diatonic and based on simple *arpeggios* (broken chords), the melodies of this second subject are chromatic. Their unstable tonality gives them a curiously fretful quality that can aptly be called "tipsy anxiety." Shostakovich had an uncanny ability to express every degree of feigned happiness or false cheer, and here you have one of his most potent examples. The waltz rises to a couple of bitingly shrill, woodwind-laden climaxes, before subsiding into an exhausted but pensive calm on the strings. Once again, the motto appears in its inverted form—a motive of three descending notes—as part of the violin melody that brings the exposition to a close.

The entire development section up to and continuing through the recapitulation of the first subject is, as previously suggested, one of the most impressively sustained passages that Shostakovich ever wrote. It is a true development in the classical sense. He doesn't just repeat his themes louder, softer, or with different scoring, but reimagines their expressive possibilities, takes them apart, and from their constituent elements constructs new ideas and phrases of every imaginable variety. And all of this happens as part of a steady increase in excitement and tension. The episode begins on bassoons and contrabassoon, recalling the motto and the clarinet theme. Other instruments gradually join in, until bits of the second subject second subject appear in the woodwinds atop the violins' forte entrance.

A crescendo on suspended cymbal reintroduces the motto theme in the bass, alternating with the waltz on trumpets, until a crash on the tam-tam leads to all-out panic. Horns blast out the clarinet theme in their high register, and variations on this melody pass from section to section until the violins at last take over the motto, which immediately descends back into its usual low position (trombones and basses) at the entry of the snare drum. The main climax consists of bits of the clarinet tune separated by horns playing the inverted motto, with each phrase accented by a crash on the tam-tam and a crescendo on suspended cymbals. This is, in fact, an expanded version of the first subject's initial climax, which you will notice immediately if you recall the role of the horns in presenting the upside-down version of the motto at its first appearance.

The remainder of the recapitulation (a varied repeat of the clarinet melody) continues at full power in steady eighth notes in the violins. The mood is no longer tragic or desperate but full of surging confidence, as the music once again achieves a horn-led climax, this time much closer in shape to the one the first time around. As the strings wind down, the trombone chorale intervenes, signaling the reprise of the second subject. This turns out to be a duet for two clarinets singing in thirds, their sweet harmony even more strangely at odds with the chromaticism of the tune than before. The second subject of the Second Cello Concerto offers something very similar.

Once this bittersweet recollection has run its course, a solo timpani roll initiates the coda, which features the motto under gleaming woodwind chords. The opening string paragraph from the very beginning of the symphony returns in its original form, leading not to the clarinet theme as expected but to a serene variant on two solo piccolos. A last reference to the motto in the lower strings leaves the movement to expire gently, in the piccolo's softly played but brightly piercing tones.

Second Movement: Allegro

The most famous movement in the symphony, this is Shostakovich's "portrait of Stalin," a graphic descent into madness that just happens to be one of the most exciting and physically exhilarating pieces of music ever written. There are no significant instrumental solos: the whole movement is written for the full orchestra almost throughout. Its entire thematic substance comes from the motto theme, announced right at the beginning by the strings and expanded into an up-and-down arpeggio by the woodwinds. The form of the movement is a simple ABA, with the B section beginning after the first series of cymbal crashes. It consists of maniacally wailing strings alternating with gibbering woodwinds, while bassoon and basses makes evil noises below them in jagged rhythms. This passage builds in fury with the addition of the percussion (bass drum, cymbals, and snare drum) in a steady crescendo.

The return to the opening themes is even more ferocious, as the heavy brass play the initial woodwind theme in long (or augmented) notes, first on the trombones and tuba, then on the horns and trumpets. Solo timpani hammer out the two repeated notes of this passage's climactic phrase, a (coincidental?) reference to the first subject of the "Leningrad" Symphony and a version of the inverted motto as well. The strings then race away with the remainder of the A section, softly at first, until a rapid crescendo brings the brass back in with a series of hair-raising fanfares and a last reprise of the motto, which brings the piece to a brilliant close. It's worth pointing out, incidentally, that all the climaxes in this movement occur in bright major keys, suggesting not just evil run amok but the genuine *triumph* of evil run amok. These celebratory moments beg the question of what it is exactly that is being celebrated, making the music all the more disturbing and gripping as a result.

Third Movement: Allegretto

The tempo designation here is deceptive: the music has the character of a slow movement despite a couple of lively outbursts. It begins with a tune on violins closely related to the Scherzo of Violin Concerto No. 1, only much slower. More to the point, this theme begins with the three rising notes of the motto, from which it clearly derives, and lives in the same emotional world as the tune that opens the second movement of the Seventh Symphony as well. In short, it's vintage Shostakovich in that emotionally ambivalent, "hear no evil, see no evil" mode that no other composer has ever tapped to quite the same degree (Mahler knew it also). Formally, this movement is a combination of sonata, with two well-differentiated main subjects, and rondo, with the opening theme returning between sections.

The second subject, scored for the entire wind section with timpani and triangle, is a wistful merry-go-round waltz containing Shostakovich's own four-note musical acronym (between the pairs of three repeated notes).* The theme passes to the violins accompanied by the remaining strings, and winds down as a trio for flute and two clarinets. When the opening melody returns, it's largely scored as originally, for strings, only with the even more shadowy addition of soft thuds from the bass drum, snare drum, and cymbals. Cellos and basses appear to be leading once again to the waltz but are interrupted by a five-note horn call. This enigmatic gesture, which opens the movement's development section, brings to mind the equally horn-led climaxes of the first movement, and sure enough, the first measures of the symphony return on the cellos and basses, as at the beginning.

This horn call has occasioned some controversy in the Shostakovich literature. It has been suggested that it represents

---

* For an explanation of how this works, see the chapter on Violin Concerto No. 1.

yet another sort of musical acronym, that of Elmira Nazirova, a Russian composer with whom Shostakovich was supposedly enamored during the composition of the symphony. Aside from the alphabetical and linguistic contortions necessary to substantiate this theory, it demonstrates with singular point the worthlessness of so much Shostakovich scholarship. Even if this motive does stand for Elmira, what does it add to our understanding of the music's expressive meaning? The answer is: Nothing. Furthermore, on two of its twelve repetitions over the course of the movement, it has six notes instead of five. Did Shostakovich forget Elmira's middle initial? Never mind. The motive does, however, sound like the principal idea from John Williams's score to *Close Encounters of the Third Kind*.

After the reprise of the symphony's first few measures, the horn call interrupts once again, followed by a bit of waltz (note the inverted motto in the clarinet), then the horn call, and a gentle wave of arabesques for flute and piccolo over dark string chords. The next two repetitions of the horn call, over a pizzicato accompaniment, consist of its six-note version, but it immediately reverts back to original form, and with the addition of soft strokes on the tam-tam, the recapitulation begins with the opening theme on the English horn, eventually joined by the oboe. Suddenly, the merry-go-round waltz erupts in the full orchestra, with emphatic percussion including tambourine, and charges forward in a vigorous passage of additional development that includes the only statement of the opening theme at full volume.

As the excitement increases, the Shostakovich four-note acronym (DSCH) takes over with hysterical repetitions interrupted by loud blasts of the horn call. This has a calming effect and initiates a bleak coda in which bits of the opening theme, the horn call, soft tam-tam strokes, and quiet thuds from bass drum and timpani tiptoe to a close. Shostakovich gives the final word to his own motive, timidly chirped out three times by flute and piccolo. This moody, deliberately enigmatic movement perfectly offsets the almost shattering intensity of the first two, and in turn offers the ideal pretext for the emotional resolution that Shostakovich reserves for the finale.

Fourth Movement: Andante–Allegro

The finale opens with a slow introduction similar in mood to the Nocturne of the First Violin Concerto, but it serves the same structural purpose as in symphonies of the classical period: to introduce a principal theme that is too light in tone and texture to lead off the movement all by itself. Beginning with a groping theme on cellos and basses, the introduction consists largely of woodwind arabesques similar to those in the development section of the previous movement. The gentle rhythm of the clarinet—dum, dadum—turns out to be the leading motive of the allegro's main theme, which takes off like a shot after a few minutes of pensive, atmospheric meditation.

Like the first movement, this finale uses sonata form, with two different subjects, but there are some special features to its themes. The first allegro tune consists of feathery light, speeded-up, happy versions of the woodwind arabesques from the introduction. This alternates with another motive containing two repetitions of a four-note, rapidly rising scale (in sixteenths) followed by two pairs of slurred rising eighth notes. It derives from the symphony's motto and has an independent existence, associating itself with the first and second subjects more or less at will.

The second subject is a gruff Russian dance on the strings, with cellos and basses offering yet another tune in three-note phrases deriving from the motto, both right side up as well as upside down. This subsidiary idea bears a striking resemblance to the main theme of the second movement, and as the development section progresses, what seems at first like the mere ghost of that movement takes on increasing substance. Suddenly, with a crash on the cymbals, evil returns amid swirling woodwinds and militant snare drum, but its triumph is short lived. At full force, the entire orchestra blasts out the DSCH acronym, capped by the cymbals and a huge whack on bass drum and tam-tam.

For me this gesture, more than any other, confirms both the meaning of the second movement and the expressive point of the symphony. Stalin's death gave Shostakovich hope for the future, and he expresses it in the most personal way: by using his own musical motive to deal a deathblow to his vision of terror. The recapitulation opens with a return to the introduction, but warmer and purged of fear. As the music of the second movement slinks away to reminders of the DSCH motive, a jocular bassoon returns with the opening theme of the allegro, and from here on, the music rushes to a joyous conclusion in which the horns and the composer's acronym become ever more prominent and rambunctious among the parade of themes already heard. The very last bars recall those of those second movement, only this time the triumph is genuine and wholly positive.

This finale represents a true musical summing up of the entire symphony: its motto theme, the most important ideas from earlier movements, and the emphasis on horns and clarinets as distinctive tone colors. At the same time, the joyous conclusion completes the work's expressive journey, and whatever one's personal feeling about what the music means in a biographical sense, it seems to me inconceivable that the symphony would have taken on its present form had Stalin not died when he did. This piece, like its two predecessors, also has a chamber-music partner in the Tenth String Quartet (1964). The tunes are naturally different, but the emotional ambiance and large-scale structure—consider

Symphony No. 10

the quartet's allegretto furioso second movement—are often curiously similar. With this great work, Shostakovich takes leave of traditional, "abstract" symphonic form for a time. His next contributions to the genre will be written for the most part along very different lines.

Part 4

Late-Period Works

Symphony No. 11 ("The Year 1905")
1957

Orchestration: piccolo, 3 flutes, 2 oboes, English horn, 3 clarinets, bass clarinet, 3 bassoons, contrabassoon, 3 trumpets, 4 horns, 3 trombones, tuba, timpani, triangle, snare drum, bass drum, cymbals, bells, tam-tam, xylophone, celesta, 2–4 harps, strings

There are many ways in which to view the Eleventh Symphony, which has been gaining steadily in popularity as a result of its innate tunefulness, atmosphere, and colorfully cinematic style. Some see its programmatic basis as a step backwards after the formal mastery of the Tenth. Others regard it as an ideological betrayal, an embrace of the tenets of Socialist Realism and a sop to the authorities, or even as a response to the events of the 1956 Hungarian uprising (Shostakovich suggested as much to his inner circle). Some or all of these theories may have some basis in truth; there are no clear-cut answers. By the same token, none satisfactorily explains what the work sounds like and expresses. So I prefer to look at the question as a musical one.

It's entirely possible Shostakovich believed that the Tenth Symphony represented a culmination of what he felt he could do with traditional forms as he understood them. I find it significant that although he was no longer the subject of the vicious purges of the thirties and forties, he nevertheless turned to entirely new and different formal solutions in his next four symphonies, combining movements and using themes in unusual ways, and also setting texts for the first time since the experimental Second and Third. He did not need to take this particular path; certainly given his fame and reputation, not to mention the death of Stalin and ensuing cultural "thaw," he might have gone on writing more of the same, but that was never his approach to composition. However personal the actual musical language employed, Shostakovich never mechanically repeats himself.

With the Eleventh Symphony, Shostakovich's late period begins, and within the context of his very characteristic individual style, he seemed determined that it not be "more of the same." That he found himself at a kind of artistic crossroads in the midfifties is supported by the biographical evidence as well. In 1954 his first wife, Nina, died suddenly, leaving him alone with two children. His mother died the following year, and shortly thereafter he entered into a disastrously hasty second marriage that ended in divorce in 1959. These events undoubtedly affected his creativity, although exactly how and to what degree we can never really know. Already in 1956, the year of his remarriage, he acknowledged in a letter to his pupil Kara Karayev (a very talented and little-known composer in his own right) that he felt himself to be written out, bereft of inspiration for new works.

This was a bit of an exaggeration. Shostakovich was a composer who needed to be working constantly, and in addition to several important film scores (including his music for *The Gadfly*, now very popular in concert form), he also completed the Sixth Quartet during this period, so he had hardly been idle. But it's interesting that he does mention the Tenth Symphony as the point at which his artistic crisis began, almost as if what was giving him the most trouble was the specific problem of how best to move forward with writing his next work in the medium. Whatever the reality of the situation, by 1957 the Eleventh Symphony was completed, and it differs in one overwhelming respect from all of its predecessors: it's the first Shostakovich symphony that ends in a mood of frightening, unambiguous tragedy.

First Movement: The Palace Square (ABABCBA)

A. "Palace Square" Music
B. "Listen" ("The night is dark as an act of betrayal, as a tyrant's conscience.")
C. "The Prisoner" ("The walls of the prison are strong . . . the gate fastened by a pair of iron locks.")

Although nominally divided into separate movements, the symphony plays continuously, and none of its sections adopts traditional forms (the Eleventh Quartet of 1966 behaves similarly). Throughout the work, Shostakovich uses the melodies of several revolutionary songs whose texts would have been familiar to contemporary audiences, but the importance of this has been exaggerated. I certainly don't know them and don't miss them when I hear the symphony, and you won't either. The return of this symphony to general favor among Shostakovich scholars and audiences has nothing to do with understanding the music's verbal subtext and everything to do with a greater appreciation in recent decades for film music in general, including Shostakovich's.

Still, it would be a mistake to regard the work as a "film score without a film," despite its clear similarities to his work for the cinema. Only the second movement purportedly depicts an actual event: the massacre by the Czar's guard of a group of peaceful demonstrators gathered in the palace square to make a point of the aristocracy's indifference to their suffering. The other three movements tell no story, and despite the quotations of formerly well-known tunes, the thematic glue that holds the work together consists entirely of original music, designated in this discussion by the letters A, D, and E. So in describing each section, I have listed not only the most important of the songs that Shostakovich quotes but also the order of their recurring appearances throughout the symphony.

The first movement functions as a long introduction to the tragic events depicted in the second. Often, because the music is so atmospheric, it's played too slowly, making it a much too long introduction, a temptation that conductors should steel themselves to resist. Shostakovich's "palace square" idea (A) actually consists of three distinct motives: the haunting strain for divided strings and harps that opens the symphony, a fanfare for muted trumpet over a soft snare-drum roll, and an ominous timpani motive in steady triplets. The mood is misty, cold, and threatening. These elements alternate for a few minutes, and then, as the timpani continue beneath, the first of the revolutionary songs (B), "Listen," appears in the flutes. The palace-square music returns, very lightly varied, and then "Listen" is repeated, this time in muted trumpets and horns, rising to a more energetic climax, after which the tune moves to lower strings.

The lyrical climax of the movement is a setting of the song "The Prisoner" (C), initially presented by cellos and basses, then played with increasing intensity by the full woodwind section. But all of the more passionate outbursts in this movement are short lived. The music swiftly subsides as Shostakovich gives "Listen" to the bassoons, instruments whose doleful timbre somehow suits the melody particularly well. A last, lingering reprise of the palace-square music brings the movement to its dark conclusion, after which the next part begins without a pause.

Second Movement: The Ninth of January ([DE]AFAEAB)

Letters in parenthesis refer to larger sections based on themes in rapid alternation or in combination.

D. "Oh Czar, Our Little Father" from *Ten Choruses on Texts by Revolutionary Poets,* Op. 88
E. "Bare Your Heads on This Sad Day" from *Ten Choruses on Texts by Revolutionary Poets,* Op. 88
F. "Massacre" Fugue

One of the advantages of writing a symphony containing a mixture of original material and preexisting tunes is that you can design the new stuff with the old in mind. In this particular case, both "Oh Czar, Our Little Father" (D) and "Bare Your Heads on this Sad Day" (E) seem to derive from the opening palace-square music, although in terms of compositional chronology, the truth is just the opposite. In addition, Shostakovich makes each appearance of "Listen" end with a chain of descending sequences, another characteristic both of "Oh Czar, Our Little Father" and "Funeral March of the Workers" (G) in the next movement. The result gives the entire work an organic unity that goes a long way towards making up for the absence of more traditional forms of symphonic development.

The entire opening section is based on "Oh Czar, Our Little Father," as both melody and accompaniment. Beginning in the lower strings, Shostakovich works this up to a powerful climax, with cymbal crashes and the tune in the trumpets. As this subsides, to persistent interjections from the snare drum, the brass section softly intones "Bare Your Heads on this Sad Day" as a mournful chorale. This entire complex is then varied and repeated, reaching an even more violent, cymbal-laden culmination. The variety that Shostakovich wrests from these two simple ideas—which get repeated relentlessly and threateningly what seems like a million times over the course of the movement's first ten minutes or so—is really quite amazing. As the second big musical wave passes, pizzicato strings take over "Oh Czar, Our Little Father," accompanied by soft rumblings from timpani, bass, and snare drums.

The palace-square music abruptly returns, now evocatively scored for the entire woodwind section in widely spaced chords: a return to earth, to a specific time and place, after the initial depiction of suffering and unrest. Suddenly the snare drum interrupts loudly, and the strings begin a terrifying, violent fugue (F) based on the timpani motive from the palace-square music. As the fugue mounts through the orchestra, brass yelps and crescendos on suspended cymbals raise the level of tension to the breaking point. With a crash on the tam-tam and brutal rhythms from the various drums, the massacre begins with the palace-square music screamed out by the full orchestra, culminating in a fortissimo statement of "Bare Your Heads on this Sad Day." The crushing sounds of percussion continue past the point where the rest of the orchestra stops, and then without warning—silence.

Or not quite: it is "the sound of silence." The palace-square music returns, close to its original form, but the differences are significant. First of all, the muted strings play trills instead of sustained notes, and Shostakovich adds a celesta to double the harp, giving the passage an icy coldness even more gaunt and grim than initially. The use of the celesta to represent this kind of chill desolation likely originated with Mahler (Sixth Symphony), and you can also find it in Benjamin Britten's opera *The Turn of the Screw*, where it symbolizes the evil allure of the two dead servants. This string texture, or something very similar, will feature in several later works by Shostakovich, including the

Twelfth and Thirteenth Symphonies, as well as the film scores *Five Days—Five Nights* and *Hamlet* (The Story of Horatio and the Ghost). Wherever it appears, its meaning is unmistakable: terror and dread.

Shostakovich recapitulates enough of the original palace-square music to include a reprise of "Listen" on the flutes, and then with a last fragment of "Oh Czar, Our Little Father" from harp and celesta, the movement slowly fades into the briefest of silences.

Third Movement: Eternal Memory (GHEG)

G. "Funeral March of the Workers" ("You fell as victims in battle, with unselfish love for the people.")
H. "Hail, Free Word of Liberty"

Glum pizzicato cellos and basses introduce the beautiful, elegiac "Funeral March of the Workers" (G), a tune often used in the Soviet cinema and one that, as noted previously, contains in its first phrases those descending sequences (four notes instead of three) initially presented in the first movement at the end of "Listen." The melody glides along at a steady, low dynamic—muted, as if in a state of emotional shock. It's worth pointing out in this connection that despite his reputation for writing music depicting a hysterical frenzy of grief and suffering, Shostakovich understood very well the value of emotional understatement, of sadness simply expressed. His treatment of the tune here offers a classic example of his sensitivity in this respect.

"Hail, Free Word of Liberty" now enters as a funeral march in the brass, accompanied by the descending motive from the end of "Listen" and "Oh Czar, Our Little Father." This is Shostakovich at his most Mahlerian, and in particular, the Mahler of the first movement of the Fifth Symphony. Violins take up the tune in a more hopeful vein and, together with the rest of the orchestra, rise to a huge climax, atop which "Bare Your Heads on this Sad Day" appears as a scorching indictment against the perpetrators of the massacre. Over roiling string triplets, the woodwinds scream out bits of "Funeral March of the Workers," and the music gradually drains of tension in time for one further reprise of that melody on the violas, exactly as it first appeared.

Finale: The Tocsin (or Alarm) ([IE]D[AE]DE)

Letters in parenthesis refer to larger sections based on themes in rapid alternation or in combination.

I. "Rage, Tyrants" ("Rage, you tyrants, mock us!") and "Varshavianka" ("Hostile whirlwinds surround us . . . The fateful battle against our enemies has begun.")

The initial section of the finale is based on several tunes, of which two of the most prominent are "Rage, Tyrants" and "Varshavianka" (collectively, letter I). "Bare Your Heads on this Sad Day" also gets tossed in for good measure, but the entire first few minutes form a sort of march fantasia in rapid tempo with these and other previously heard themes variously presented, so there's no point in worrying about which melody appears where. The bold opening passage, particularly the writing for cellos and basses, once again reveals the legacy of Mahler: specifically, the first movement of the Second Symphony and the finale of the Sixth. This is particularly true of the lengthy marching passage for triple-forte strings, which might have come straight out of the latter work.

This first section, after more than a few brass-led perorations, reaches its climax with frantic string triplets recalling the moments leading up the massacre episode in the second movement, after which "Oh Czar, Our Little Father" makes yet another trumpet-led appearance. A huge crash from cymbals and bass drum cuts off the march, and for the last time, Shostakovich takes us back to the palace square. Atop the now familiar stillness of strings and harps, a solo English horn presents an extended meditation on "Bare Your Heads on this Sad Day."

Suddenly, threatening thuds on the tam-tam and drums wake the specter of "Oh Czar, Our Little Father" on the lower woodwinds: the timbre of the bass clarinet is wonderfully evil here, but "Bare Your Heads on this Sad Day" has the last word. It rises through the orchestra to the brass section via horns, strings, and xylophone, over a relentless snare-drum rhythm punctuated by the clangor of alarm bells and massive crashes from the cymbals and tam-tam. In this state of high panic, with the bass drum reinforcing the snare-drum rhythm, the symphony stops abruptly, leaving the last tones of the bells hanging in the air.

Although it outwardly reflects the dictates of the Socialist Realist aesthetic, the Eleventh Symphony is in fact the darkest and most tragic of all of Shostakovich's purely orchestral works. It dwells almost entirely in minor keys, certainly more so than any of his nonprogrammatic preceding symphonies, and no other work of his so relentlessly sustains an atmosphere of dread, suffering, and violence. It is, in this sense, almost a stereotypical example of what all of Shostakovich's music is commonly assumed to be about; but heard in context, its single-minded intensity not only becomes all the more impressive in itself but also reveals just how expressively varied and diverse the other symphonies actually are. For this reason alone, it plays an important role in any understanding of Shostakovich's symphonic achievement as a whole.

Piano Concerto No. 2
1957

Orchestration: solo piano, piccolo, 2 flutes, 2 oboes, 2 clarinets, 2 bassoons, 4 horns, timpani, snare drum, strings

Although Shostakovich reportedly derided this piece as "without substance," that's not a judgment to be taken without a big grain of salt. I find it highly unlikely that he would write something for performance by his own son Maxim, dedicate it to him, and then advertise the fact that it's junk. On the other hand, if by this opinion he meant "light and lacking in seriousness," then he had a point, for this is his most charming and unprepossessing major work. Playing for less than twenty minutes, neoclassical in form as well as in both wit and polish, this concerto stands—with the equally delightful piano concertos of Poulenc and Ravel (in G Major)—among the most enjoyable and entertaining twentieth-century works in the form. The fact that it's easy to play and often sounds wonderful when interpreted by pianists of the second rank (including the composer), often showing up in pops concerts as a consequence, really should be seen as a point in its favor.

First Movement: Allegro

As in all of Shostakovich's concertos, the soloist plays from the very start. After a few introductory bars on the woodwinds, the piano chimes in with a jocular main theme in the shape of a carefree march. The first subject of this almost traditional (you'll see the reason for the "almost" in a moment) sonata-form movement follows an ABA pattern, the middle section being one of those *William Tell* overture gallops that appear so frequently in Shostakovich's work. This leads to a grand restatement of the opening theme for piano and orchestra. The full sonorities that Shostakovich gets from his small ensemble really are remarkable for their amplitude and color.

The second subject, lyrical and just a touch elegiac, dwells on wistful minor keys. It's announced by the piano in octaves, to a gentle rhythmic accompaniment in the strings, and leads directly into the development section, which consists primarily of variations on the two parts of the first subject in alternation between piano and orchestra. At its culmination, Shostakovich triumphantly presents the second subject in the full orchestra in long notes (the piano accompanies), leading to a dashing and very fast solo cadenza that initiates the recapitulation in dialogue between piano and woodwinds.

Now comes the "almost." There is no formal recapitulation of the second subject at all. Shostakovich builds the movement to a rapid climax based on the *William Tell* gallop, and with just the merest hint of the second theme in a bright major key, the movement comes to a brilliant and punctual close. It's a strategy perfectly suited to an opening movement in quick tempo of particularly light character.

Second Movement: Andante

This lovely movement is a simple verse-and-refrain in ABABA form, where the first idea is a soulful strain for muted strings and the second is a gorgeous melody for piano over a "Moonlight

Sonata" accompaniment in triplets. Once the piano starts, it keeps up that triplet rhythm for the remainder of the movement, playing straight through the remaining sections, each subtly varied on repetition. Aside from a few quiet, almost inaudible low notes on a single horn, only the strings play, a gentle reminder of the early classical-period practice of dropping the winds in slow movements. The most remarkable thing about this melodically gorgeous movement is how uncharacteristically warm and romantic it sounds, proving that Shostakovich could have written his serious music in a more conventional melodic style had he so chosen. In fact, his film scores abound in this sort of writing, and you can even hear a miniature romantic piano concerto in *The Unforgettable Year—1919* (1951).

Finale: Allegro

The finale follows without a break. It's another gallop, full of verve, but the most interesting melodic idea in the movement is the second subject, with its curiously uneven rhythm of 7/8 (that is, seven beats per measure). This irregular meter, combined with the dazzling scoring for woodwinds, makes an unforgettable impression. The development section concerns itself primarily with this ear-catching second subject in dialogue between piano and orchestra, while the recapitulation features a rhythmically altered version of the opening tune on piano that gives it additional weight and impact. Shostakovich adds snare drum to the reprise of the second subject, and then piano and orchestra join forces in a dazzling coda that brings the work to a close at high speed.

There's no need to comment further about this immaculately crafted piece. Even though it doesn't stand among Shostakovich's most emotionally searching works, he clearly lavished no small bit of care over the details. The music is very easy on the ear but also formally quite successful, and it won't do to underestimate just how difficult it is to compose well in a light style. In fact, Shostakovich was an excellent composer in this vein, as his numerous ballet and film suites attest. It is especially interesting that both of his piano concertos number among his least serious works, and both were very much family affairs, the first for himself, the second for his son.

Cello Concerto No. 1
1959

Orchestration: solo cello, piccolo, 2 flutes, 2 oboes, 2 clarinets, 2 bassoons, contrabassoon, 1 horn, timpani, celesta, strings

It's reported that when asked what his First Cello Concerto was "about," Shostakovich impishly replied, "I just took a simple, tiny theme and tried to develop it." The result is arguably the finest cello concerto of the twentieth century, one of the very few to withstand comparison to the greatest work in the medium: Dvořák's. It is also quite possibly the most neurotic piece that Shostakovich ever wrote, and that's saying a lot. The principal emotional characteristic of the outer movements is a twitchy, obsessive, nervous anxiety that's as unforgettable as it is disturbing. The music really gets under your skin, while never forgetting the need to display the virtuosity of the soloist in an effective and satisfying way. Given the fact that it was written for legendary Russian cellist and conductor Mstislav Rostropovich, it could hardly be otherwise.

Rostropovich notes that the proximate inspiration for the Cello Concerto was Prokofiev's sprawling and neglected Sinfonia Concertante (Symphony-Concerto) for Cello and Orchestra, a piece that in recent years has enjoyed a number of fine recordings, even if it has yet to earn a regular place in the concert repertoire. Both works exploit the high register of the cello very imaginatively, but otherwise they have little in common and certainly sound more like their respective composers than they do each other. The orchestration of the Shostakovich, in particular, is exceptionally skillful and refined, with important solo roles given not just to the cello but also to the single French horn and, remarkably, the timpani.

First Movement: Allegretto

That "simple, tiny theme" with which the cello opens the concerto is a four-note motive similar in character to Shostakovich's DSCH musical monogram. In other words, it is chromatic and therefore harmonically unstable. The orchestra, on the other hand, has a simple *William Tell* overture jogging rhythm consisting of pure major chords, and this creates a tension between melody and accompaniment that Shostakovich very imaginatively exploits throughout the movement. For the first several pages of score, Shostakovich pits the cello against the woodwind section. Pay particular attention to the gravelly contributions of the bassoons and contrabassoon, which give the music such an ominous undertow. Everything about this music is tense and edgy: the harmony, rhythm, and orchestration, and it's about to become more so.

This movement is written in pellucidly clear sonata form, like the first movement of the Ninth Symphony, with very cleanly differentiated first and second subjects, and the same tempo maintained throughout. There are no breaks between sections. The second subject begins with loud timpani thwacks answered by a jerky rhythm in the woodwinds. Against constantly shifting meters that more or less add up to an irregular 5/2 pulse, the cello sings out one of Shostakovich's "Jewish" themes. Its first strain hovers around a single note, and the second phrase, broken by brief interjections from the orchestra, tries to dance but never quite gets off the ground. The cello writing rises higher and higher in both range and frenetic energy, until it gradually subsides, and a sour version of the second subject on solo clarinet brings the exposition to a close.

The development section has an ABA form, beginning with the first subject's four-note theme on solo horn. The rest of the orchestra takes this up by degrees, against a steady accompaniment in running eighth notes on the cello. Then the winds take over, sounding like gibbering lunatics, while the cello honks away petulantly at the opening phrase of the second subject. It is music of absolute, obstinate madness, at once funny and frightening. The solo horn returns with the first subject, passing it on eventually to the cello, which initiates the recapitulation exactly as at the beginning of the piece. The second subject, however, concentrates on the two protagonists almost exclusively: solo cello plays the broken-rhythm woodwind figure, while the horn get the tune, sounding just as strained in its high register as did the cello the first time around.

After the horn finishes, the melody passes back to the cello, which leads in diminuendo to a coda based on the first subject. The music seems about to subside into dark muttering, when a last bang on the timpani and a reminder of the second theme brings the music to an abrupt halt. It is very difficult to capture in words the effect of this music, at once witty, grotesque, and uncomfortable. Stravinsky's assistant and biographer Robert Craft, who encountered Shostakovich on a visit to Russia, described him as one of the most nervous people he had ever met. Hearing this movement, it's easy to understand exactly what he meant. It sounds like the musical equivalent of an uncontrollable tic.

Second Movement: Moderato

It's tempting to take this movement, like so much of Shostakovich's music, too slowly, but the "moderate" tempo indication means what it says. Conductors and soloists need to remember that this extensive piece is followed by the largely meditative and very lengthy cadenza, which needs to be perceived (at least initially) as a moment of absolute stillness. So this moderato should flow. Keeping the music moving also helps clarify the form, which is a brilliant and sophisticated combination of sonata and rondo somewhat similar in shape to the finale of the Eighth Symphony. In practical terms, this means the following structure: ABA–development (C)–AB. Both the ritornello theme (A) and the second subject (B) are quite easy to distinguish, being assigned to the orchestra and the solo cello respectively.

There is nothing of the grotesque in this movement. The contrabassoon does not participate, and the piccolo has only a few notes at the movement's climax, in octave unison with the flute. The tone colors here are dark and warm, with special emphasis given to the consoling timbre of the full string section. They play the opening melody, a soothing chorale that vaguely resembles the beginning of Dvořák's "New World" Symphony. The horn soon joins in and brings this first paragraph to a gentle close that overlaps the entry of the cello. This theme is one of the most beautiful in all of Shostakovich, a hauntingly sad lullaby whose repeated notes and rocking motives may remind you of the "Jewish" second subject of the first movement. As in that previous melody, a solo clarinet takes the tune over from the cello on its immediate repetition.

A last bit of melody from the cello leads back to the opening chorale, which segues smoothly into the development section as the soloist takes over and expands on the idea first given to the horn. This in turn introduces a wonderfully tender variation of the lullaby, gently accompanied by squeezebox chords from flute, clarinets, and bassoons. With masterfully planned gradations in volume, the cello develops this idea into a passionate climax for the (almost) full orchestra, culminating in a single stroke on the timpani and the fortissimo return of the chorale. Once again the horn participates, as at the beginning, but the second subject is rescored for cello harmonics and celesta over a delicate thread of wandering violin tone. It is the most ghostly, ethereal sound imaginable, perhaps inspired by the conclusion to Mahler's *Songs on the Death of Children* (*Kindertotenlieder*). In this atmosphere of fragile calm, the music runs directly into the:

Third Movement: Cadenza
Fourth Movement: Allegro con moto

As with the First Violin Concerto, the cadenza is so large that it effectively merits its own movement designation. Shostakovich did not do so in the earlier work, but he does here, as this particular example is even longer than its predecessor. Indeed, at about six minutes on average, it's bigger than the actual finale. It also serves a dual function: to continue the development of many of the themes heard so far and to provide a gradual transition from the transfigured calm of the moderato to the high-spirited insanity of the finale. Such a long passage for the soloist would fall apart if it did not have a distinct form of its own, although one which never weakens the improvisatory character that defines a cadenza in the first place. All you need to know is that it has four sections, separated from each other by a refrain of pizzicato chords. These sections increase in both speed and musical density as they proceed, until the accumulated energy spills over into the finale itself.

Like the corresponding movement in the First Violin Concerto, this is a short rondo. It has a very classical (as in

Haydn and Mozart) form: ABACA—coda. You can also hear that Shostakovich has remembered his lesson from the earlier work written for David Oistrakh and given the soloist a rest after the cadenza by having the wind section play the opening theme of the finale. This tune, like that of the first movement, is chromatic; and the accompaniment, in hollow fifths, is if possible even more disturbingly askew. It further has elements that bear a striking resemblance to the "massacre" fugue in the Eleventh Symphony. Each statement of the theme ends with a four-note commentary from the timpani. Something very similar in mood will also characterize the scherzo of the Fifteenth Symphony.

The first episode, following a brilliant downward scale from the woodwinds, is a dashing virtuosic melody for the cello against which the timpanist keeps up his four-note interjections, although a bit less obtrusively. Against a rapid figuration from the cello, the opening ritornello returns as previously, in the woodwinds, leading quickly to the next episode—a desperately bitter waltz in the strings, then cello. Shostakovich retains the triple-time waltz rhythm for the final return of the ritornello and gives it to the violins fortissimo and *feroce* (ferocious), while the accompaniment in fifths grates even more tellingly as it rises from the basses to the upper register of the second violins.

Suddenly the woodwinds scream out the four-note motive that opened the concerto. The strings respond with their galloping rhythm, and the coda begins. The solo horn gets a hold of the motive, and then the cello restates the entire theme, ultimately in combination with the finale's ritornello on the woodwinds. The remainder of the movement is all brilliant finish, with the horn and woodwinds blasting out the four-note motive as the soloist's high-speed passagework dashes into the gleeful final bars. With its manic mood swings and extreme contrasts between heartfelt lyricism and caustic wit, this is not just a great cello concerto but one of Shostakovich's best works in any medium.

Symphony No. 12 ("The Year 1917")

1961

Orchestration: piccolo, 3 flutes, 3 oboes, 3 clarinets, 3 bassoons, contrabassoon, 3 trumpets, 4 horns, 3 trombones, tuba, timpani, triangle, snare drum, bass drum, cymbals, tam-tam, strings

The Twelfth Symphony has the distinction of being widely regarded as Shostakovich's worst. Certainly the Second and Third are probably even less popular, and they are without doubt more difficult to grasp, but they are also youthful experiments and thus excusable on those grounds alone. Prior to composing the Twelfth, Shostakovich went through a terrible personal crisis, the origins of which remain obscure. He had just joined the Communist party (in 1960), something he clearly did not wish to do and a decision regarded as an act of betrayal by fellow members of the artistic intelligentsia. Apparently he even considered suicide, and his tormented state of mind can be heard in the dark and turbulent, clearly autobiographical Eighth String Quartet, with its use of his musical acronym and its numerous quotations from his own most important works.

For years he had been under pressure, not just to join the party, but to write a grand symphony in Lenin's memory. In his official statements, he insisted that he was working on such a project, but somehow it never materialized. It may well be he thought that in the Eleventh Symphony he had paid his debt to the aesthetics of Socialist Realism, but that work was seen as too dark and too tragic, despite its revolutionary program. It contained too much realism and not enough socialism, but it was a totally straightforward work in the sense that the music clearly did exactly what the movement titles suggested. In the Twelfth Symphony, none of the movements lives up to its programmatic billing, a fact that is so obvious it has to be intentional.

Circumstantial evidence suggests that at least Shostakovich did manage to buy a little artistic peace with the Twelfth. He never wrote another work like it (save for the late symphonic poem *October,* of 1967), and his subsequent three symphonies are about as subversive as he could make them. The same holds true for the late song cycles, such as *Satires,* composed at just this time. I'm certainly not going to rock the critical boat and claim that this symphony is a neglected masterpiece. That's a matter for each listener to decide individually. But it does contain quite a bit of good, characteristic music. And because Shostakovich's idiom is so expressively accurate, the mere act of listening to it with his other works in mind reveals more of his musical intentions than any amount of biographical speculation.

Like the Eleventh Symphony, the Twelfth is in four connected movements, but unlike its predecessor, these largely employ traditional forms. What is more, the entire piece is based on a single theme announced right at the start. These facts should tell the attentive listener right away that compared to the Eleventh, the music exists independently of any programmatic explanation and has its own business to mind. Note also the comparatively restrained scoring: no English horn, bass clarinet, harps, celesta, or exotic percussion. The emphasis clearly isn't going to be on instrumental color for its own sake but rather on thematic transformation and development. This symphony is also quite compact, running for less than forty minutes on average. So let's see just what gets transformed and developed and, in the process, try to figure out what it means.

First Movement: Revolutionary Petrograd (Moderato–Allegro)

In terms of sound and harmonic idiom, this is Shostakovich's most traditional symphony, a deliberate homage to the nineteenth-century romantic tradition. It opens with a very Russian motto theme for strings, much like Borodin's Second Symphony, and this tune serves as the basis for almost all the ensuing melodic material throughout the work. The process of simple thematic transformation, such as you can also hear in the Eleventh Symphony, is put to use in the service of a sonata-form opening movement. The introduction moves steadily to a climax for full orchestra in six-note phrases, separated by pauses and capped with a percussive crash from bass drum, tam-tam, and snare drum. Then the allegro takes off at full speed.

The tune of the introduction becomes a quick march, the mood and texture very similar to that of the second and fourth movements of the Eleventh Symphony and also the "Stalin" scherzo of the Tenth. Shostakovich builds the tension swiftly to an exciting, cymbal-capped return of the main theme in its original form, followed by an impressive diminuendo. Beginning in the lower strings, the second subject is optimistic, although still clearly derived from the music of the introduction. It reaches a jubilant and brassy climax in tones familiar from such works as the popular *Festive Overture,* but at the height of the celebration, a whack on the tam-tam sends the orchestra careening into the development section.

Some commentators note that Shostakovich's treatment of sonata form in this movement is "free," in that the development and recapitulation are not regular. The fact is that sonata-form movements are *always* "free" if the composer knows what he is doing, because they take their shape from the nature of the thematic material itself. In this case, since all the tunes have a common source, and the movement will flow without pause into the next one, which is also based on the same material, there's no need for a strict treatment of form. It would only sound pedantically stiff. The development accordingly begins with anxious music that actually quotes the Eleventh Symphony's "massacre" fugue and creates an impression of general turmoil, amid which both first and second subjects come and go. What this has to do with revolutionary Petrograd is anyone's guess, but the sustained agitation and energy are impressive. It's really exiting stuff.

After several minutes of increasingly intense tumult, the music finds itself back at the conclusion of the introduction, and the movement self-destructs to the same percussive crash as launched the allegro. Now comes what passes for both recapitulation and coda, as Shostakovich reviews for one last time the main thematic material, only in reverse order, with the second subject appearing first. At the same time, the dynamics steadily decrease, and the mood calms. Pay particular attention to the tiny three-note figure played pizzicato by the lower strings. It's derived from second, third, and fourth notes of the symphony's opening, and it turns out to be quite important as the work proceeds.

Second Movement: "Razliv" (Adagio)

Razliv is the name of Lenin's hideout prior to his emergence to lead the Bolshevik revolution. Again, the actual course of the music says nothing obvious that might connect it to that locale; indeed, it's difficult to imagine what a programmatic representation of the place should sound like. There is, however, a strong conceptual relationship in style, mood, and texture to a composer very close to Shostakovich's heart, particularly at this time in his life: Mussorgsky. In 1940 he had reorchestrated the opera *Boris Godunov,* and in 1959 he prepared what is now the standard performing edition of *Khovantschina,* arranging its variously complete fragments and scoring it from scratch. He would shortly (in 1962) orchestrate the *Songs and Dances of Death* for soprano Galina Vishnevskaya. Shostakovich took a great deal of pride in his work on these projects, designating each with one of his own opus numbers.

Mussorgsky's operas describe with unvarnished honesty the suffering of the Russian people and the tragedy of a country torn by oppression and misrule. There is no question that Shostakovich saw himself not just as a composer but as a chronicler, documenting the history of Soviet Russia in tones—in terms not of what happened specifically but how it felt to experience life under that authoritarian regime. This is not, of course, the sum total of what Shostakovich's music is, but it remains an important element. In the slow movement of this symphony, he comes closest to Mussorgsky, and specifically to act 1, scene 1 of *Boris Godunov,* which describes the monk Pimen writing his history of Russia, a hidden document containing the truth of Boris's crimes in usurping power. With him is Grigory, also a monk and soon to become the next pretender to the throne.

The correspondence between the two pieces is remarkable, even though the Mussorgsky is an opera with text, and the symphony has no words. It certainly seems to, though: the instrumental writing gives the impression of monologue and dialogue. In the opera, the scene opens with a lonely, wandering figure in the strings that stops periodically as Pimen reflects on the approaching conclusion of his historical work. "Razliv" opens with a similar motive, also in the strings, derived from the motto theme. Over this, various instruments play a fragment of a tune familiar from the Eleventh Symphony, "Bare Your Heads on this Sad Day" from Shostakovich's *Ten Choruses on Texts by Revolutionary Poets,* Op. 88. Each statement of this melody concludes with a brief liturgical chorale, like the chanting of the monks offstage in Mussorgsky's opera. You will also hear the three-note pizzicato motive from the end of the previous movement interrupting the music's flow now and then.

This slow movement has a simple ABA form, and the initial A section presents varied combinations of the wandering strings, the "Bare Your Heads" tune, and the chorale four times in all, the latter scored for horns, strings alone, strings and woodwinds, and finally the brass: trumpets, trombones, and tuba. The first movement's second subject also appears in the lower strings, revealing its close kinship with the thematic material of its surroundings. The central B section is a tranquil tune in irregular rhythm for flute and clarinet over soft string chords. It also has a distinctly chantlike, almost ecclesiastical tone, especially when taken over by the bassoon. The wandering motive returns on solo clarinet, followed again by a snatch of the B melody and then the chorale.

If the kinship to *Boris Godunov* seems doubtful up to this point, it is about to become much less so. Soft beats on the tam-tam reintroduce the wandering figure in the clarinet. In the opera, these tam-tam strokes represent the tolling of the matins bell. Over feverish string tremolos, a trombone intones an extended recitative based on "Bare Your Heads," a texture virtually identical to Grigory's outburst at the end of the scene. The words he sings are:

> Boris! Boris! Before you everything trembles.
> No one even dares to mention the fate of the child.

> And meanwhile, a hermit in a dark cell is writing a fearsome indictment of you:
> You will not escape the people's judgment,
> Just as you will not escape God's judgment.

The movement draws to a close with fragments of the central flute and clarinet theme and more of the three-note pizzicato motive.

Of course, the relationship between *Boris Godunov* and this movement is mere speculation, but it has the virtue of being based on easily audible musical facts. "Razliv" is also the first in a new kind of Shostakovich slow movement, one very characteristic of his late symphonies in general. The music's hushed, desolate quality; the thematic material based on gently oscillating string textures; and the spare orchestration will all feature prominently in the next three symphonies. As if in compensation for the overall mood of bleakness, there's also a certain melodic tenderness, a sweetness, that similarly becomes an important part of the composer's late idiom. You will hear this as well in the works to come, a moment of easeful lyricism just when the darkness appears most potent.

Third Movement: "Aurora" (Allegro)

Guns fired from the battleship Aurora signaled the assault on the Winter Palace at the beginning of the Bolshevik coup, and they are represented in stylized fashion by a percussive salvo at the end of this movement somewhat similar to the "massacre" music in the Eleventh Symphony. Otherwise this brief interlude has no independent existence in terms of form or content. It consists almost entirely of the flute and clarinet theme from the previous movement's central episode. Played in a quick tempo, as here, by pizzicato strings, later joined by woodwinds, its irregular rhythms acquire a very surprising level of tension. As this first wave subsides, shadowy strings are joined by one of Shostakovich's "terror" motives: a soft stroke on the tam-tam followed by a bass-drum roll. This will reappear in the fourth movement ("Fears") of the next symphony.

Under all of this, the first movement's optimistic second subject appears in the bass trombone and tuba, rising through the orchestra with increasing urgency, until the percussion fusillade begins and the entire orchestra blasts out the flute and clarinet tune from "Razliv." Again, what it all "means" in a programmatic sense, aside from a generic cannonade, is anyone's guess, but it's a pretty nifty bit of thematic transformation. Indeed, moments such as this become more impressive the better one knows the symphony, and unfortunately its reputation as a poor work prevents most listeners from taking the time to enjoy its musical highpoints—of which, I hope you can see, it has quite a few. As far as this passage goes, it accomplishes the same sort of "darkness to light" transition as the corresponding link from third to fourth movement in Beethoven's Fifth Symphony.

Fourth Movement: "The Dawn of Humanity" (Allegro–Allegretto)

The ridiculous title of this movement ought to prove to all sensible listeners the silliness of any programmatic interpretation of this music. The very suggestion that Shostakovich believed for one second that his finale represented a musical embodiment of "the dawn of humanity" is simply too absurd to bear further consideration. That he expected the party hacks to accept the noisy conclusion and title at face value, which they apparently did, should come as no surprise, but to call the symphony a failure because the music doesn't live up to its impossible descriptive heading really is to miss the entire musical sense of the piece. This final rondo is in fact one of the most "abstract" movements that Shostakovich ever wrote, a purely formal summing up of the content heard so far. It just so happens to be mostly in a major key, and it ends triumphantly (sort of), but whatever a "dawn of humanity" sounds like, it's safe to say that this ain't it.

Like most classical rondos, this one has the basic form ABACA. The ritornello theme (A), which emerges from the climax of "Aurora," is a majestic idea for horns, once again clearly based on the symphony's introductory motto. It glides on majestically to a cymbal-capped climax, after which the tempo switches to allegretto, and a vivacious triple-time episode begins. This is mostly quiet, playful music close in character to the finale of the Eighth Symphony, although without that work's fragility and bitter edge. The motto theme pops up now and then, its minor key providing an effective contrast to the general mood of contentment. The ritornello soon reappears in the original tempo, again on the horn, now accompanied by pizzicato strings with plenty of those three-note figures so prominent in the first and second movements. It reaches yet another brief climax, but after a couple of cymbal crashes, the tempo increases and the second episode begins.

This next section has one purpose: to combine the motto theme with the first movement's frantic initial allegro, its optimistic second subject, and finally the ritornello as well. These elements pile up in a huge climax that stops short, and the three-note motive (now in timpani) introduces a moderato coda that does double-duty for the final A section of the rondo as well. First the motto theme returns in the strings, recalling for the last time the broken phrases that ended the symphony's introduction.

Then the first movement's second subject chimes in, followed by the ritornello in the trombones, all the while interspersed with three-note figures that chop up the phrases.

The last word actually goes to the flute and clarinet theme from "Razliv"'s central episode (and the percussive climax of "Aurora"). Whether this particular victory impresses you as unambiguously happy, merely bombastic and superficial, or something in between depends to a large extent on how much conviction the players bring to it. Done in classic Russian fashion (that is, louder than hell), as Shostakovich expected, it's pretty impressive no matter what it may represent, and certainly no more embarrassing than the similarly grandiose conclusions to such symphonies as Tchaikovsky's First or Copland's Third.

In other words, what Shostakovich actually wrote here is a full-blown romantic symphony in a four-movements-in-one form, similar to such works as Liszt's B Minor Piano Sonata. He then passed the result off as an essay in party-line Socialist Realism, which it most definitely is not, by adding a few titles and dedicating the result to Lenin's memory. In fact, it is the music's formal concision and expressive abstraction that makes the ruse possible in the first place. Shostakovich was incapable of composing a lie; his idiom, like Mussorgsky's, was simply too emotionally accurate and clear-cut in mood for that. But he could write one kind of music, pure and self-contained, and call it something else. The result may be atypical: a "safe" work that avoids extremes of comedy and tragedy—but that doesn't make it bad music.

Symphony No. 13 ("Babi Yar")
1962

Orchestration: piccolo, 2 flutes, 3 oboes, English horn, E-flat clarinet, 3 clarinets, bass clarinet, 3 bassoons, contrabassoon, 3 trumpets, 4 horns, 3 trombones, tuba, timpani, triangle, snare drum, bass drum, cymbals, tam-tam, woodblock, castanets, whip, tambourine, glockenspiel, xylophone, bells, 2–4 harps, piano, celesta, strings, bass solo, male choir (40–100 basses)

The early 1960s saw the relaunch of Shostakovich's banned opera *Lady Macbeth of Mtsensk District* (now revised to take some of the edge off and named after its antiheroine, *Katerina Ismailova*), as well as the long-delayed premiere of the Fourth Symphony. Shostakovich would have loved to write more operas. It's not well known to any but hard-core fans, but in 1959 he wrote an excellent musical comedy called *Moskva Cheremushki* that was quite successful in its day both on stage and in a movie version. His dramatic instincts and gift for musical characterization have always been acknowledged as among his great strengths, and his extensive work in film and incidental music for the theater had honed these skills even further. For whatever reason—lack of a suitable libretto or just plain fear—he never fulfilled his operatic ambitions, but the late vocal works, including the Thirteenth and Fourteenth Symphonies, go a long way towards making amends.

Indeed, during the last decade and a half of his life, Shostakovich created a number of impressive pieces for a wide array of vocal and instrumental forces, including *Satires* (1960), *The Execution of Stepan Razin* (1964), *Seven Blok Songs* (1967), *Six Songs by Marina Tsvetayeva* (1973), *Suite on Verses by Michelangelo Buonarroti* (1974), and *Four Verses by Captain Lebyadkin* (1975). Many of these texts reveal clearly dissident or subversive content, and it's a sign of Shostakovich's increasing confidence in his position that he devoted so much of his remaining energy to the setting of words. And make no mistake: it was an effort. Throughout this period he was increasingly ill, plagued by a degenerative nerve disease said to be a rare form of polio, and also the victim of both heart attacks and, finally, inoperable lung cancer. Although happily remarried since the early 1960s to a loving and supportive woman, it soon became evident that he was dying. That knowledge, if anything, gave Shostakovich's music even more directness and intensity than ever before.

The circumstances surrounding the first performance of the Thirteenth Symphony remain the stuff of legend. Government pressure caused two prospective bass soloists to withdraw, one at the very last minute. Fortunately Vitaly Gromadsky, the "just in case" understudy, was able to step in at the dress rehearsal. Right up to the moment of the premiere, pressure to cancel was put on conductor Kyrill Kondrashin. Yevgeny Mravinsky, Shostakovich's lifelong supporter and music director of the Leningrad Philharmonic, declined the chance to unveil the new work, whether from party pressure, fear of reprisals, latent anti-Semitism, or a combination of the three. This slap in the face to Shostakovich hurt him terribly. The work was "unofficially" banned immediately after the premiere, and the score had to be smuggled out of the country by cellist Mstislav Rostropovich so that it could be safely played in the West.

Adding insult to injury, author Yevgeny Yevtushenko, fearful of government displeasure, immediately produced a revised version of the opening movement's poem, "Babi Yar," one that added numerous lines about others besides Jews suffering the ravages of war. Shostakovich was horrified, made a few half-hearted changes to the text, and this is the version Kyrill Kondrashin was forced to use in the work's first official recording five years later (the original version has long since been restored). In short, the piece caused a major scandal, and if there had been any speculation that the Communist party had crushed Shostakovich's spirit, this symphony erased it once and for all.

First Movement: "Babi Yar" (Adagio)

One of the outstanding qualities of this symphony is the simplicity and clarity of its text settings. All-vocal symphonies, sung throughout, date back to Mahler's Eighth of 1907 and include *A Sea Symphony* by Ralph Vaughan Williams (1909) and Benjamin Britten's *Spring Symphony* (1949). This is the first, however, to employ a single bass soloist backed by a chorus of basses, a dark and particularly Russian sound. The chorus sings for the most part entirely in unison, and there is no complex vocal counterpoint or layering of parts at all. When Shostakovich does use polyphony, as in the finale's fugue, the context is purely orchestral, a fact that reveals another important point: the music's expressive directness rests on an extremely sophisticated and tightly wound formal infrastructure, one that supports Shostakovich's designation of the piece as a true symphony rather than a cantata or song cycle. This first movement, for example, follows Shostakovich's patented brand of slow sonata form, and achieves an effortless, organic fusion between its large-scale shape and the necessary moment-by-moment musical illustration of the meaning of the words.

Babi Yar is a ravine near Kiev, Ukraine, where in September 1941 the Nazi SS shot and killed approximately 34,000 Jewish men, women, and children. Yevtushenko's poem takes this event as its starting point, proceeding to document centuries of anti-Semitism in the world at large and in Russia (then including Ukraine) particularly. This criticism of Soviet society, one still unfortunately relevant, was bound to attract Shostakovich, who regarded anti-Semitism as one of history's great evils and who actively identified himself with the persecution of the Jewish people. As a victim of vilification in his own right, he knew (and more importantly, felt) the suffering described in Yevtushenko's poem with particular acuity, as well as sympathy.

Here is a brief outline of the movement's formal structure, although as with all texted music, the best way to listen is to follow the words as they are sung:

Exposition

This section has two well-defined thematic complexes, corresponding to the two principal images evoked in the text. The symphony opens with a motto, the "Babi Yar" theme, beginning with a rising, chromatic, four-note slither over a plodding pizzicato bass, all introduced by a tolling bell. Bits of this theme and the sound of the chime will return throughout the symphony as a reminder of its most important image: the empty ravine, scene of unimaginable atrocity, over which no monument sits because the victims were Jews. The chorus and bass soloist expound on this image, citing past victims of anti-Semitism, from Jesus to Dreyfus to a little boy caught up in the Bialystok pogrom of June 1906.

The poem itself couldn't be more graphic; "I am held captive, surrounded, persecuted, spat on, and slandered . . . " According to soprano Galina Vishnevskaya, who was present when Shostakovich played through the completed work for the first time, these words held a special, personal significance for the composer. The tempo increases slightly for the second subject: over a vulgar "oompah" accompaniment of tuba and pizzicato strings, punctuated by a cold descending four-note woodwind phrase (the "Babi Yar" motive turned upside down), the chorus describes a drunken mob bent on brutalizing Jews to "save" Russia. The violence is indiscriminate, coarse, and graphically detailed: "A grain-merchant beats up my mother!" the chorus shouts as blaring brass bring this section, and the exposition itself, to an uneasy close after a rapid diminuendo.

Development

The development section follows the general course of the exposition, expanding its main ideas in response to the imagery of the poem. It begins with a hazy recollection of the symphony's opening, now on violins gently reinforced by celesta but with the tolling bell omnipresent. The bass soloist then enters with a passionate plea to the Russian people not to allow their good name to be sullied by sloganeering anti-Semites who buy national unity with the coin of hatred. This last thought reintroduces the chorus and a bit of the second subject to hammer home the point, immediately interrupted by the soloist, imagining Anne Frank, young and beautiful and full of hope, refusing to see the forces of evil on the march. These creep in stealthily, continuing the development of the second subject, transforming it into one of those rapacious and terrifying marches familiar from the first movements of the Fifth and Eighth Symphonies.

Recapitulation

As is so often the case with Shostakovich's sonata-form movements, the climax of the development section serves as the opening of the recapitulation. The "Babi Yar" theme returns full force, its tolling bell now the sound of an alarm, with militant snare-drum rolls and huge crashes on the tam-tam. Strings and woodwinds swirl above the tune in the brass like a malevolent, destructive storm of Biblical proportions. The passage reaches a tremendous climax that collapses with a crushing blow from the bell, tam-tam, and bass drum. Out of the reverberant haze of percussion, the chorus emerges with its opening theme, slightly modified to take into account the different words. The imagery, however, returning to the contemplation of Babi Yar itself, is similar to that at the beginning of the symphony, and so this recapitulation encompasses both the music and the actual sense of the text.

Since the latter stages of the development concerned themselves so extensively with the second subject, Shostakovich omits it here, as he does in the emotionally very different finale of the Fifth Symphony and first movement of the Second Piano Concerto. These three examples reveal just how expressively flexible Shostakovich's handling of form actually is. Like all great composers, he uses the sonata style as a blank canvas on which he can explore the widest range of moods and feelings.

In this case, the coda begins in a mood both hopeful and heroic with the reentry of the chorus looking forward to the day when the last anti-Semite has been buried. The bass amplifies this thought further: he is hated as though he were Jewish himself, and this is what makes him (the chorus joins in) "a true Russian." With these words, the orchestra rises to one last climax of the "Babi Yar" motive: the clanging bell and other crashing percussion march the music full force to its startlingly abrupt close.

Second Movement: "Humor" (Allegretto)

Shostakovich's late works have a reputation for being morbid and death obsessed, but the fact is that his symphonic "dark night of the soul" is the avowedly Socialist Realist Eleventh Symphony. The finale of the Twelfth shows him recapturing some elements of playfulness, while in the last three symphonies (even the otherwise grim Fourteenth), humor makes a welcome reappearance, and Yevtushenko's poem goes a long way towards explaining why. Humor is an inherently subversive element—irrepressible, immortal, and humbling even czars, kings, and emperors. The lightheartedness of the words finds its formal analogue in a rambunctious rondo, having the classic ABACA shape, with a brief coda based on a tune from the C episode. Pay special attention to the rising string figures at the very beginning, derived from the "Babi Yar" motive with which the symphony began (stretched out to five notes instead of four).

Yevtushenko's poem describes humor as a sort of prankster, much like Richard Strauss's Till Eulenspiegel from the eponymous symphonic poem, always playing tricks on the authorities, and it's interesting to note that Strauss's work is also in rondo form (he uses the old French spelling: *rondeau*). The reason is very logical: the episodes separating the appearances of the opening ritornello really *are* "episodes" in the narrative sense, describing humorous events. Shostakovich's ritornello is pure film music, similar in character to such pieces as the "Folk Festival" from the score to *The Gadfly* and full of brilliant high-pitched sounds: woodwinds, triangle, and tambourine. The first episode details humor's ability to make the rich seem "like beggars" and to deflate hypocrisy, demolishing pretentiousness "like pieces on a chessboard."

A crack of the whip, a very characteristic percussion sonority in Shostakovich from this symphony onwards, signals the first return of the ritornello. The next episode (C) is the longest and has three parts, two vocal narrations enclosing a central orchestral interlude. Each of these stories describes the vain attempt to murder humor: first, by chopping his head off and sticking it onto a soldier's pike. This event initiates a mocking reprise of the actual "Babi Yar" theme on high woodwinds, complete with its original call to attention from the tubular chime. But humor springs back to life and strikes up a merry dance, initially for violins with jingling triangle. This latter tune has a double meaning. It comes from "McPherson's Farewell," a very famous poem by Robert Burns about the man of the title's upcoming execution. The text has a long and illustrious history as a folk song: Haydn even made an arrangement of it. Shostakovich set the text as one of his *Six Songs (Romances) by Raleigh, Burns and Shakespeare* (1942). Its refrain is singularly apt:

> Sae rantingly, sae wantonly,
> Sae dauntingly gae'd he:
> He play'd a spring, and danc'd it round,
> Below the gallows-tree.

Shostakovich's original theme for this song belongs to his family of "Jewish" dance melodies, one of those tunes whose happiness comes to sound increasingly desperate as it proceeds. A crash on the tam-tam and another crack of the whip introduces the second attempt to murder humor, this time as a political prisoner, and once again the "Babi Yar" music returns, more fearsomely than before, only to be further mocked by McPherson's dance below the gallows-tree. This leads back to the ritornello, a final reprise that points up the moral of the story: Humor is "eternal. He's artful. He's quick-witted. He survives everybody and everything. So all hail to humor! He's a brave fellow." And to a short coda based on "McPherson's Farewell," capped by a last whip-crack, the music drives to its dashing, music hall–style close.

Third Movement: "At the Store" (Adagio)

The remaining three movements are linked, not just because the music plays continuously, but by the gently wandering "motto" theme in cellos and basses with which the third movement begins. Interestingly, this tune not only recalls the main idea of the Twelfth Symphony's slow movement, it is actually a dark transformation of the heroic horn melody that opens that work's finale. The resemblance is so close that it cannot be accidental, and it sheds further interesting light on the Twelfth's avowedly Socialist Realist intentions. It's almost as if Shostakovich is saying: "See what the 1917 revolution truly achieved. The 'dawn of humanity' may have been the ideal, but this bleak variation is today's Soviet reality."

Yestushenko's poem is a tribute to Russian women, symbolized by their patient waiting in line at a store. The music is heartbreakingly tender and compassionate but also bleak, punctuated by one of the most desolate sounds that Shostakovich ever devised: a simple tapping rhythm on castanets and woodblock. This motive is closely related to the "ticking clock" music of the Fourth and Fifteenth Symphonies, and the Second Cello Concerto. It poignantly evokes passing time—a lonely, inexorable emptiness—and it will return appropriately to conclude the Fourteenth Symphony as well.

Formally this movement follows a simple pattern of alternation between solo and chorus, with small variations of each repeated section, until the last time around, the vocal forces unite in a huge climax, with the opening theme appearing high in the violins for the very first time, like a cry of pain. The text condemns those who try to cheat the waiting women, and the passage concludes with a lacerating series of sharp chords punctuated by cracks of the whip, music that returns in Shostakovich's film score to *Hamlet*. Something quite similar will also appear in the song "Creativity" from the *Suite on Verses by Michelangelo Buonarroti*. As the movement concludes, the soloist sings of the women's "saintly hands," and for the first time, the chorus breaks into harmony, with a solemn musical "amen." The wandering theme returns again, as at the start on cellos and basses, leading without a pause to the:

Fourth Movement: "Fears" (Largo)

This is music of suffocating terror, but you may have heard something like it before: first, in the very similar opening to the finale of Mahler's Sixth Symphony and, more pertinently, in the third movement, "Aurora," of the Twelfth Symphony. One of the elements that Shostakovich learned from Mahler was that of the musical *gesture,* often consisting of a simple noise from the percussion section or a brief chord or cluster of notes almost too short even to be called a motive. This symphony is littered with them: the tolling bell, the tapping rhythm on woodblock and castanets in the previous movement, and now, from the Twelfth Symphony, a soft stroke on the tam-tam followed by a hairpin crescendo on bass drum. It's a chilling sound, particularly when accompanied, as here, by the tuba's hollow, aimless solo. Cellos and basses repeat their motto theme, followed once again by the tuba and percussion complex. Then the voices enter in a monotone, muttering "Fears are dying in Russia," but the music clearly says otherwise.

The form of this movement, ABACDAEA, resembles that of a rondo, but the course of the music never gives the impression of clear sections separated from each other by appearances of the motto theme (A) as a well-defined ritornello. Rather, this melody flows along beneath the poem as a unifying element. The initial vocal entry of the soloist (B) describes Stalin's reign of terror, first to ominous rhythms from the opening movement in bassoon and bass clarinet, and then, after another gesture of terror from tam-tam and bass drum along with the motto theme, to (C) muted but militant fanfares on woodwinds and brass. These rise to a brief climax punctuated by a loud stroke of the bell. Ghostly trills, like those following the Eleventh Symphony's massacre episode, accompany the fear of speaking to strangers—even to one's own wife (D). The motto theme threads through this passage as well, as the trills subside.

Meanwhile, the piano has begun a steady tread in its lowest register (E). Accompanied by strings struck with the wood of their bows (*col legno*), the chorus recounts how fearlessly the Russian people worked in blizzards and died in battle, only to become mortally afraid of each other. The soloist, to whirling strings and bright glockenspiel chords, adds a list of new, healthier fears, including that of "dishonestly disparaging ideas which are self-evidently true." The music rushes to its biggest climax yet, a direct return to the "Babi Yar" first subject of the opening movement. With a fearsome crash on bass drum, tam-tam, and whip, followed by a loud stroke of the bell, the music subsides into darkness (and the motto theme), with the poet fearing that he has not written his words at full strength.

Fifth Movement: "A Career" (Allegretto)

The flute duet that opens this finale constitutes one of the most marvelous thematic transformations in all of Shostakovich. It is in fact nothing more than the motto theme, now easeful, mellow, and purged of all darkness and anxiety. If you want to hear this more clearly, simply listen to the first few seconds of the third movement, then skip to the fifth. A lyrical oboe solo reinforces the music's pastoral character. Unlike the previous movement, this one really is a rondo, just like "Humor," having the shape ABACA. Moreover, the second (C) episode also consists of two vocal sections framing an instrumental interlude containing one of Shostakovich's "Jewish" tunes. The form is even more sharply defined in this case because the ritornello—that is, the motto theme in this new version—always appears exclusively in the orchestra, while the voices only participate in the two episodes. The music of these episodes is delightful: playful and childlike, like the similar sections of the finale of the Twelfth Symphony.

The text of the entire poem (in my own free translation) is worth quoting, because it might well serve as Shostakovich's artistic credo:

[opening statement of the ritornello (A) as a flute duet]

(B episode)

> The priests insisted that Galileo was foolish and dangerous,
> But as time showed, the fool was the wiser.
> One scientist, a contemporary, was no stupider than Galileo.
> He too knew that the earth revolved, but he had a family.
>
> As he got into his carriage with his wife, having accomplished his betrayal,
> He thought he had advanced his career, but in fact he destroyed it.
> Galileo faced the risk alone, and for his discovery about our planet,
> He became a great man.
> This is what I understand as being a "careerist."

[orchestral ritornello (A) on pizzicato strings]

(C episode)

> And so all hail a career, when it's a career like Shakespeare's, or Pasteur's,

Newton's, or Tolstoy's—(Leo?) Leo!
Why was dirt thrown at them? Talent is talent, however it's called.
They're forgotten, the ones who were doing the cursing,
But we remember the ones that they cursed at.

[orchestral fugue]

All those who reached for the stratosphere,
The doctors who died of cholera,
That is what it means to have careers!

I take their careers as my example.
I believe in their sacred belief,
And this belief is my courage.
I make my own career, then,
By not making it!

[orchestral ritornello (A) on solo violins, then coda]

The subject of the fugue is actually the theme sung by the bass at his first very first entrance. By modifying its first four notes and turning them into a rising chromatic phrase, Shostakovich introduces one last reminder of the "Babi Yar" motive as the solo and chorus sing "I take their careers as my example." Then the music gradually goes to sleep, one of those timeless "infinity" endings familiar from the Fourth and Eighth Symphonies. The transformed motto theme returns on two solo violins, marking the final appearance of the ritornello, and yields at last to a music-box conclusion in the form of the fugue subject on celesta, evaporating one phrase at a time, until a last tap on the chime ends the symphony in a mood of perfect peace and contentment.

If you love this magnificent and deeply moving work particularly, as I do, you'll be pleased to know that it even has a sequel: *The Execution of Stepan Razin* (1964), called by Shostakovich a "poem for bass, mixed chorus, and orchestra." The text is also by

Yevtushenko, the music recognizably of the same stripe as that of the Thirteenth Symphony. This thrilling thirty-minute work, one of the least known of Shostakovich's major statements, also belongs in any serious collection of his orchestral pieces.

Cello Concerto No. 2
1966

Orchestration: solo cello, piccolo, flute, 2 oboes, 2 clarinets, 3 bassoons, contrabassoon, 2 horns, timpani, whip, woodblock, tom-tom, tambourine, snare drum, bass drum, xylophone, 2 harps, strings

There's an unavoidable prejudice attached to anything called "No. 2," particularly when "No. 1" is universally considered to be one of the greatest works in its medium, as is the case with Shostakovich's First Cello Concerto (and First Violin Concerto, for that matter). Toss in the music's unusual approach to form; its sparse, late-period style; and the fact that it ends quietly, and the result constitutes a virtual kiss of death as far as wider popularity is concerned. Nevertheless, the Second Cello Concerto is a magnificent piece, full of beautiful and arresting ideas, imaginatively presented. Its emotional range is typically wide, but its communicative intimacy will always mean that it's a work best suited to connoisseurs. Having decided to read this book, you are now officially a connoisseur—but honestly, all the music asks for is close, sympathetic listening.

Shostakovich wrote this concerto in the spring of 1966, just before his first heart attack, as a sixtieth-birthday present to himself. So while the dedication to cellist Mstislav Rostropovich provides the proximate source of the work's inspiration, the musical content is not only personal (all of Shostakovich's music is that), but it's probably safe to assume that it is at least to some extent autobiographical as well. Still, this is a very different composer than the one you hear in the Fifth Symphony. The tone is darker in some respects, but the music is also more lyrical and graceful, and there's an underlying sweetness and simplicity to many of its themes that's both surprising and affecting. Toss in the colorful, utterly transparent orchestration, and the result is music of very special character.

First Movement: Largo

This movement uses Shostakovich's personal brand of slow sonata form, here adapted to the concerto medium. You will find the expected two subjects, but because both are introduced by the solo cello and employ *chromatic* (i.e., "colored" or dissonant) harmony, like the opening of the First Violin Concerto, the differences between the various themes are subtle rather than obvious. This sets into high relief the more rapidly moving development section, and as you will see in considering the finale, there's a very good reason for this. The subdued tone of this opening is typical of late Shostakovich, with a shadowy main theme similar to ideas you can hear in the Second Violin Concerto (first movement), Twelfth Symphony (second movement), Thirteenth Symphony (third movement), and Fourteenth Symphony (first song, "De profundis").

The first four notes of the concerto, a pair of identical two-note descending motives played by the cello, function as a sort of motto for the entire work. Shostakovich immediately begins growing a long, wandering theme that incorporates them. Chromatic melodies such as this are always difficult to remember at first pass. They impression they give, especially at slow tempos, is one of wistful longing and sadness, but Shostakovich takes great care to firm up the rhythm and harmony at crucial points such as the moment where he turns the opening four notes upside down to create a rising figure at the melodic climax of the first musical paragraph. Note the menacing entrance of the woodwinds with yet another version of the main tune, accompanied by pizzicato cello. This event signals the end of the first subject.

The second subject begins, once again, with the cello presenting the theme, now lightly accompanied by strings and harp, with gentle interjections from the horn. You can always recognize this idea, because it's less a melody than a simple series of notes harmonized in thirds. Like the similar writing in the Tenth Symphony's first movement, this gentle consonance sits uneasily in such a highly unstable, chromatic context, and the contrast between the two kinds of harmony is very typical of Shostakovich's late style. The opening of the First Cello Concerto makes a great deal out of this same principle. This new theme also contains the four-note motto, highlighted with some particularly arresting harmony so that you can catch the fact. But that doesn't make this piece monothematic, as in the Fifth Symphony. The second subject is without question a different musical idea, with some shared elements embedded within it.

On the other hand, like that of the Fifth, this development section moves at a decidedly faster pace. Shostakovich simply starts writing in shorter note-values, and this gives the impression of doubling the tempo. Beginning with tapping xylophone and flecks of woodwind (you can hear something quite similar in the second subject of the Second Violin Concerto's opening movement), the music now begins to dance. The tune comes from the opening melody. The dance grows increasingly wild until the second subject appears at the climax in the horns and strings. The woodwinds all the while continue their whirling figurations above, interrupted at irregular intervals by the solo cello, like a person trying to shout above an increasingly unruly crowd.

A thud on the bass drum stops the orchestra dead in its tracks, while the solo cello, despite the persistent drum thwacks, finally gives voice to a richly passionate version of the second subject. As the passage dies down, cellos and basses signal a return to the concerto's opening, and a highly compressed recapitulation begins. The first subject lasts only a few bars, because after a much more extensive restatement of the second subject by the cello, strings, and harp, Shostakovich returns to the dancelike development of the opening theme for the movement's coda. But the music lacks the energy to continue dancing for long: the final word belongs to the second subject, with a rustle from the harp and the horn tossing in the four-note motto at the very end.

Second Movement: Allegretto

This nutty piece is based on the Ukrainian street vendor's song "Bubliki, Kupitye Bubliki," which might be translated as "Bagels! Buy Your Bagels!" And just like bagels, this tune belongs to the large collection of Jewish-style melodies that began infiltrating many of Shostakovich's major works from the 1940s on. You can find them in the First Violin Concerto, First Cello Concerto, and Thirteenth Symphony, as well as numerous chamber works and, of course, the song cycle *From Jewish Folk Poetry*. Shostakovich loved these tunes, feeling that they expressed a bitter, forced, hollow joy. The melody also resembles another folk song of Russian origin, one that became the popular hit "Those Were the Days." It is, as you can hear for yourself, a marvelously catchy tune, whose jocularity sounds particularly strained when played in the high register of the cello.

Once again the soloist starts the movement, but pay attention to the little five-note fanfare figure right at the beginning. This will take on an independent life later and morph into an extremely important motive on solo horn, one that concludes with the concerto's initial four-note motto. A thoroughly mischievous character, this idea romps around the movement in every instrumental part, at every possible speed. As it turns out, the Ukrainian folk song itself constitutes the first subject of a very demented example of quick sonata form. The second subject, introduced by the solo cello, consists of four-note phrases ending in grotesque glissandos. It has a close counterpart in the second movement of the Sixth Symphony.

The development section begins with both the horn motive and the cello figure that preceded it (now on solo timpani). Cello and orchestra romp about with this material for a minute or so, and then Shostakovich offers a very remarkable-sounding variation of the opening melody for the soloist backed by chattering bassoons. The busyness increases, and as in the first movement of the Fifth Symphony, the climax of the development initiates the recapitulation with the folk song in the cello with a maniacal giggling accompaniment in the horns. The ensuing dash through the second subject features the solo interrupted by exclamations from the full orchestra, and then the horns take over the movement's initial fanfare figure, turning it into the real thing atop a snare-drum roll and spilling over into the:

Finale: Allegretto

This finale is so unusual in structure that I have never seen any of the popular literature (program notes, album booklets) attempt to describe it in any detail. In fact it's not all that complicated in terms of its sequence of events. The content is far more curious than the actual form, which is simply that of a fanfare introduction, tripartite theme, and four variations. In the third variation, Shostakovich begins to summarize the material of the previous movements, and he continues this overlapping of cyclical recapitulation and variation in the last of them, which also functions as a coda. That's about all there is to it.

Shostakovich wrote very few sets of orchestral variations; the first movement of the First Violin Concerto is one, very free in design, and he includes an extensive variation-style episode in the finale of the Fourth Symphony. Otherwise, he prefers to use the technique of thematic transformation within the context of other less sectional forms, and variations are simply a built-in aspect of his musical language. Here, however, he comes closest to a strict variation structure, and as you can see, it's not all that strict. This movement is also a close emotional relative of the finale of the Fifteenth Symphony, even to the point of ending almost identically. Here is its structure in outline:

Fanfare (horns and snare drum)
Cadenza-Fanfare (cello and tambourine)
Theme
Variation 1
Variation 2
Variation 3
- First subject of first movement
- Cadenza-Fanfare (cello and snare drum, then full orchestra)
- Folk song (reprise of second movement)
- Cadenza-Fanfare (cello and orchestra)

Variation 3, continued
Variation 4
- Second subject of first movement

The only other piece of information you need to understand this movement perfectly is a brief description of the theme itself. It has three elements:

1. A shockingly sweet cadence that functions as an introduction to every single variation, always played by solo cello.
2. A long, lilting melody, initially played by the harp, passing from instrument to instrument, with various counterpoints above and below. This supple, lyrical passage allows Shostakovich to morph the music into the first movement's opening theme and second subject.
3. A sardonic march for cello and percussion, differently scored each time. The solo ultimately continues the march alone, returning to the initial cadence and so beginning the next variation.

As you can see, variation 3 falls into two parts, because the big restatement of earlier music interrupts before its concluding march. This recapitulation includes not just the concerto's opening theme but also a big piece of its dancelike transformation from the first movement's development section, and this explains why Shostakovich took such pains to highlight the beginning of that passage the first time around, making it easy to recognize on its return nearly half an hour later. After the big climax, with expressionistic scoring that includes harp glissandos as well as some vicious whip cracks, Shostakovich logically picks up where he left off, continuing the third variation with its march episode—a decidedly limping version this time, over which the cello plays more bits of its first-movement opening melody.

The fourth and final variation confirms the concerto's feeling of cyclical symmetry. The sweet opening cadence yields to the expected lilting melody, now on the orchestral cellos, followed this time by the first movement's second subject, scored as originally for soloist, strings, and harp. This softly dies away to the concerto's initial motto, followed by the march on pizzicato cello. Taking up the bow one last time, the soloist lands on a single long-held note, as the percussion plays a tick-tock rhythm virtually identical to that which will conclude the Fifteenth Symphony, and which closes the scherzos of both that later work and the earlier Fourth Symphony. In fact, this piece never actually ends in the sense of finding a comfortable resolution: it simply stops. First the percussion drops out, and then the cello, noticing that everyone else is silent, makes a tiny crescendo on that single long-held note and stops too. It's the musical equivalent of a quizzical shrug.

Most commentators describe this conclusion as "enigmatic," and in a sense it is, although it becomes less so if you simply accept its sardonic sense of humor at face value. Other endings by Shostakovich similarly gaze out into infinity, suggesting a vast, empty space or time ticking away. The Fourth, Eighth, Thirteenth, and Fifteenth Symphonies all do it (more than the number of crash-bang, Fifth Symphony–type finales, in fact) but this is the only concerto in his family of six to finish quietly, in "mysterious" mode. Accordingly, the piece hasn't become, and will likely never be, as popular as the magnificent First Cello Concerto. Still, what matters most isn't frequency of performance but the fact that it's marvelous music that no one but Shostakovich could possibly have written.

Violin Concerto No. 2
1967

Orchestration: solo violin, piccolo, flute, 2 oboes, 2 clarinets, bass clarinet, 2 bassoons, contrabassoon, 4 horns, timpani, tom-tom, strings

Strike 1: It's not the First Violin Concerto, which is universally regarded as a major masterpiece.

Strike 2: It's even more difficult to play and is written in some very awkward keys for the soloist.

Strike 3: It's a very late work by Shostakovich, meaning it has a reputation for unrelieved bleakness.

No wonder this concerto is neglected! Nothing can be done about the first two strikes against it, but the third isn't true at all. Like all of Shostakovich's major works, especially the late ones, this is a serious piece, but one hardly unapproachable or excessively gloomy in tone. In fact, the first two movements are quite lyrical. It's also nicely compact, playing for an even half hour on average. Like the First Concerto, it was written for David Oistrakh, and it has more than its fair share of virtuoso fireworks, as well as some very attractive and characteristic tunes. The scoring isn't as richly colored as its predecessor, but the work's forms are particularly clear, placing it in the orbit of Shostakovich's more neoclassically inclined pieces such as the Ninth Symphony and First Cello Concerto. The music's structural and expressive straightforwardness also make it particularly easy to describe.

First Movement: Moderato

This sonata-form movement is quite well defined, not just by immediately identifiable themes, but by the fact that the two subjects of the exposition as well as the entire development section all take place in distinct tempo areas. The moderato first subject harks back to the Tenth Symphony. Beginning on cellos and basses, the violin enters above with its own lyrical theme, which becomes a seamless outpouring of melody. Sometimes the soloist and orchestral voices exchange parts, but it all culminates in a broad horn-led climax, just as did the first subject of the symphony. The quicker second subject, on the other hand, is vintage late Shostakovich: a five-note motive on woodwinds and solo violin, backed by bits of nursery tune—now on the horn, then moving from one instrument or section to the next. It's a curious mixture of fragility and innocence.

The development quickens still further to allegretto, beginning with the movement's two subjects in their original order, then variously combined. Listen for the entry of the tom-tom (a relatively high-pitched tenor drum without snares), which signals the section's beginning and interjects isolated, loud thumps at irregular intervals. The second subject has a tendency here to morph into music you might recognize, such as the four-note motive that opens the First Cello Concerto, and it carries the development to an agitated climax, culminating in a sharp exchange between the violin and pizzicato orchestral strings. Shostakovich reserves the actual moment of recapitulation for the soloist unaccompanied, playing both its initial melody and its accompaniment. The first subject continues with the gentle entry of the strings, supporting a gorgeous duet between horn and violin. Along with soft timpani beats, the horn also leads off the second subject, now a gentle shadow of its former self. With brief interjections from solo bassoon, flute, clarinet, and tom-tom, this idea brings the music to a pensive, pianissimo close.

Second Movement: Adagio

A simple ABA in shape, this slow movement opens with a haunting, slightly slithery chromatic melody for solo violin. It's a close relative of the main theme of the Twelfth Symphony's second movement, though less dark, with a more positive upward thrust. The mood of hushed meditation, though, is similar, and continues with a lovely flute solo in counterpoint to the violin. This entire first section, in fact, proceeds as a series of duets, first between violin and flute, then violin and clarinets, then violin and lower strings (which actually have the main theme). The central (B) episode begins as a long-limbed melody for violin over soft string-chords. Horn, bassoons, and oboes soon enter calmly and depart, but a soft roll on timpani introduces a violent, brief cadenza for the soloist, later accompanied by anxious tremolo strings. This leads back to the opening theme on violin, which also gets the flute's initial tune, leaving the accompaniment to cellos and basses. The last word, though, goes to another beautiful solo for the horn.

Finale: Adagio–Allegro

A classical rondo in ABACA form, this finale begins with a rhapsodic introduction whose sole purpose is to effect a transition to its amusing ritornello theme. Taking over without pause where the slow movement left off, the soloist makes a few initial gestures, then starts trading little three-note exchanges with the horns—and then it's off to the races. Each time that the ritornello returns, it will be preceded by these three-note exclamations, and you never know exactly when they will stop and the tune will start. The effect is very funny and precisely the sort of thing that Haydn loved doing in his rondos.

There's a touch of grotesquerie here, but no bitterness. The two episodes (B and C) refer back to the first movement, and the second culminates in a huge cadenza that summarizes the entire melodic and expressive content of the concerto. Even the melody from the middle movement of the Second Cello Concerto, a Ukrainian folk tune, puts in a passing appearance. At the end of the cadenza, high-pitched oboes and clarinets join the solo violin, a startling sound achieved by the simplest of means. In the dash to the finish, the violin returns to the brilliant figurations introduced at the end of the first movement's development section, before frantic glissandos and a riot of three-note hiccups slam the concerto to a dazzling close in raucous high spirits.

Symphony No. 14
1969

Orchestration: strings (10 violins, 4 violas, 3 cellos, 2 basses), castanets, woodblock, three tom-toms (high, medium, low), whip, bells, vibraphone, xylophone, celesta, soprano, bass

This is Shostakovich's most uncompromisingly grim symphony, but there's more here than the usual description of it as "eleven poems about death." Strictly speaking, the work isn't about death at all: it's about loss, protest, and defiance, and death is simply the most powerful agent of loss. Shostakovich did not believe in an afterlife. He said on more than one occasion, both in his music and to his friends, that people's deeds are all that remain after their passing, and these will determine how they will be remembered by posterity. Shostakovich also feared death and regarded it as an outrage, almost an affront—one to be opposed with all of one's strength. At the same time, he recognized that the battle cannot be won. This is the confrontational philosophy at work in the Fourteenth Symphony.

The proximate inspiration for the work was Mussorgsky's *Songs and Dances of Death,* which Shostakovich orchestrated for soprano Galina Vishnevskaya, but Mahler's *Kindertotenlieder* (Songs on the Death of Children) lurks in the background too, while the concept of a "song-symphony" finds its origins in the same composer's *Das Lied von der Erde* (The Song of the Earth).

Shostakovich dedicated the Fourteenth Symphony to British composer Benjamin Britten. It was written very quickly during a lengthy hospitalization for advancing polio, which was crippling Shostakovich's ability to move his arms and hands.

Unsure if he would live to complete it, let alone hear it performed, there's something very sobering about the image of him sitting in the hospital, reading these particular poems, and hurriedly setting them to music. So this symphony is difficult not because it is enigmatic or obscure but because it's just the opposite: harrowingly straightforward, with no time to waste on digressions or niceties. Shostakovich best described its general character to his friend Flora Litvinova, in answer to a different question entirely:

> You ask if I would have been different without "Party guidance"? Yes, almost certainly. No doubt the line that I was pursuing when I wrote the Fourth Symphony would have been stronger and sharper in my work. I would have displayed more brilliance, used more sarcasm, I could have revealed my ideas openly instead of having to resort to camouflage: I would have written more pure music. (Wilson)

Well, here he is all of those things: sharp-edged, brilliant, sarcastic, and openly revealing his ideas, damn the consequences. The mask comes off, even more than in the Thirteenth Symphony, with singularly, intentionally uncomfortable results.

The early performance history of the symphony was predictable: the party did its best to delay the premiere without outwardly banning the work. But Shostakovich was simply too famous by 1969, although the temporary unavailability of Galina Vishnevskaya resulted in a battle royal between two of Russia's greatest sopranos (the other was Margarita Miroshnikova) over which of them would have the rights to the first performance. Miroshnikova had learned the part for a private audition before a select audience of artists and party functionaries to determine if the work was "safe." It turned out not to be. One of Shostakovich's most vociferous persecutors on the Central Committee, the widely hated Pavel Apostolov, had a heart attack and died during the performance. "I didn't want *that* to happen," Shostakovich is reported to have said (Wilson).

This fortuitous event only added to the work's powerful mystique, and the result was a simultaneous double premiere, in Moscow and Leningrad, with both sopranos taking part. The choice of a female participant was a forgone conclusion, given the role Vishnevskaya played in the work's gestation. On the other hand, Shostakovich's preference for the bass voice both here and in the Thirteenth Symphony, *The Execution of Stepan Razin,* the *Michelangelo Suite,* and several other vocal works harks back to Mussorgsky and *Boris Godunov.* It's an aspect of Shostakovich's Russianness, a grand musical tradition still very much alive, in part thanks to the splendid repertoire that composers such as Shostakovich wrote for those big, dark, Russian male voices.

The orchestration also contributes much to the music's edgy brilliance, not to mention its occasional sarcasm. Note that all the percussion instruments are relatively high pitched. Despite the dark subject matter, Shostakovich omits all the usual orchestral heavy artillery: horns, trumpets, trombones, bass drum, tam-tam, timpani, and snare drum. Instead, the vibraphone makes its first appearance in the symphonies. Textures are often sparse, sharply etched, and frequently luminous. The string writing exploits the full range of the section, from the lowest notes of the basses to the most ethereal sounds of the violins. By joining various songs together and sharing a few simple ideas among them, Shostakovich creates what is in effect a five-movement symphony, lasting about forty-five minutes. As with the Thirteenth, the best way to listen is to sit down with the words, but here is a brief description of each number listing the scoring in addition to the strings:

Part 1

No. 1: "De profundis" (Lorca)–Adagio
strings only, bass

A haunting poem beginning with the line, "A hundred lovers sleep deeply under the dry earth." The setting is all top and bottom—violins, violas, and basses, but no cellos—with an opening theme closely related to the main idea that dominates the last three movements of the "Babi Yar" Symphony.

Part 2

No. 2: "Malagueña" (Lorca)–Allegretto
castanets, soprano

"Death came into and left the tavern," sings the soprano, as the music conjures up the frantic strumming of guitars, the clicking of castanets, and a desperate, demented, drunken waltz. Pay particular attention to the steady rhythmic acceleration by the accompanying strings, followed by screaming high violins, as the soprano sings "i ushla iz taverni" (and left the tavern). This accelerating motive will return to conclude the symphony.

No. 3: "Loreley" (Apollinaire after Brentano)–Allegro molto (with several changes of tempo)
whip, xylophone, woodblock, celesta, bells, vibraphone, soprano, bass

This duet tells a lengthy story, familiar from German legend, of a beautiful enchantress. Abandoned by her lover, she wishes to die, but her beauty is such that even the bishop cannot bring himself to burn her at the stake. So he has three knights escort her to a convent (galloping horses on woodblock). As they pause along the way, she throws herself off a cliff and drowns in the Rhine. The two whip cracks that open this song reappear as two strokes on the bell at the moment Loreley leaps into the river, while the image of her lying dead under the water truly is bewitching, thanks to the cool, unearthly tones of vibraphone and celesta.

No. 4: "The Suicide" (Apollinaire)–Adagio
xylophone, celesta, bells, soprano

The luminous textures that conclude the previous song reappear briefly in this one as well, including the two bell strokes at its climax. But for the most part, this sad, broken-hearted number is a beautifully spare setting for voice and solo cello. "Three lilies lie on my grave without a cross."

Part 3

No. 5: "On Watch" (Apollinaire)–Allegretto
woodblock, three tom-toms, whip, xylophone, soprano

In this kinky number, with its sarcastic xylophone solo and military rhythms in the tom-toms, the fairly obviously insane soprano sings of the impending death in battle of her brother, who is also her lover. "This is the hour of love, of feverish neuroses," she insists, as she makes herself beautiful to celebrate the moment of death.

No. 6: "Madame, look!" (Apollinaire)–Adagio
xylophone, soprano, bass

A moment of black humor: "You have lost something," says the bass. "It's just my heart," replies the soprano. "It was over there, in the trenches, but now it's back again, and I laugh loudly at the loves cut down by death." The Russian word for "laugh loudly" or "guffaw," *khokhochu,* offers Shostakovich some very graphic, onomatopoetic opportunities, assisted by a mocking xylophone. Although the tempo is adagio, the rhythm of the piece gives the impression of much quicker motion.

No. 7: "In the Santé Jail" (Apollinaire)–Adagio
woodblock, bass

A song of protest from a man falsely imprisoned, his humanity stripped from him. Strings struck with the wood of the bow (*col legno*) and a simple rhythm on the woodblock similar to that in "At the Store" from the Thirteen Symphony evolve into the strangest of all Shostakovich's fugues. This perfectly illustrates the aimless pacing of the prisoner "like a bear in a pit." The song concludes with a moving plea for pity and compassion.

Part 4

No 8: "Zaporozhye Cossacks' Reply to the Sultan of Constantinople" (Apollinaire)—Allegro
strings only, bass

A wonderfully angry, juicy string of insults full of sarcasm and malice: "You were born when your mother pathetically farted in her colic . . . " that sort of thing. There's little doubt as to why this song was included and just who the targets of Shostakovich's musical payback truly are.

No. 9: "O Delvig, Delvig!" (Küchelbecker)–Andante
strings only, bass

The lyrical soul of the symphony, this deeply affecting song features three solo cellos playing heartbreakingly sweet harmony, with light additional support from violas and basses. The text is not about death, but immortality: "What place do those with talent have among fools and criminals? . . . Where does persecution lead? Immortality is the reward for brave and noble actions, and for those who create sweet songs."

Part 5

No. 10: "The Poet's Death" (Rilke)–Largo
vibraphone, soprano

Death as release from the cares of the world: the music develops themes from the very first song, and much of the imagery (that of bodies lying in eternal sleep) is the same. The entire opening section of this number is set for soprano and violins in a gently intertwining duet. The rest of the strings enter gradually, with some light reinforcement from the vibraphone, until the texture has imperceptibly moved from the highest register of the violins to the cellos and basses—from light to darkness. The full string section utters a soft benediction at the very end, but the last word goes to the violas.

No. 11: Conclusion (Rilke)–Moderato
woodblock, castanets, medium tom-tom, soprano, bass

Both singers present the symphony's moral: "Death is great . . . He cries within us even when we believe ourselves to be surrounded by life." The texture recalls No. 7, with more of those desolate percussive clicks on woodblock and castanets (later, tom-tom), familiar from the Thirteenth Symphony's third movement. After a hair-raising climax, the strings perform one last acceleration similar to that in No. 2, ending the symphony with a violent shudder.

This symphony is sometimes performed with its texts retranslated back to their original languages. Shostakovich himself favored performances in the native tongue of the audience because he hated the sound of pages turning at concerts. There is no excuse for this on recordings. Performance in translation makes nonsense out of the rhythm of the vocal lines, and beyond that, Shostakovich's brilliance in setting Russian is one of his best-kept secrets. With its unpredictable stress patterns and abundance of liquid and soft consonants, Russian is an extremely beautiful and musical language, and the sound of the words is very much part of the musical conception.

Symphony No. 15
1971

Orchestration: piccolo, 2 flutes, 2 oboes, 2 clarinets, 2 bassoons, 2 trumpets, 4 horns, 3 trombones, tuba, timpani, triangle, castanets, woodblock, whip, high tom-tom, snare drum, bass drum, cymbals, tam-tam, xylophone, glockenspiel, vibraphone, celesta, strings

The Fifteenth Symphony is often described as enigmatic on the one hand and an intentional summing up of Shostakovich's symphonic work on the other. It seems to me that if the latter is true, and perceivable as such, then the former can hardly be true as well. There's really nothing obscure about this piece at all: its expressive message is clearly and succinctly projected, its forms equally shapely. The orchestration list above already gives a strong hint of what to expect. Note the absence of woodwind extras in the lower register: English horn, bass clarinet, and contrabassoon. The scoring comes closest to that of the Ninth Symphony, a work conspicuous for its bright colors and more than a hint of humor. You will find many similar qualities here.

The greatly enlarged percussion section—with whip, vibraphone, tom-tom, and celesta taken over from the previous symphony—also confirms Shostakovich's preference for light, airy, and luminous textures in these late works. Not that darkness is absent: far from it. But its presence generally exists in stark opposition to the brighter moments. The music similarly tends towards contrasts of top and bottom, consecutively or simultaneously but with little filler in the middle. Moments where the full orchestra participates are extremely few and far between, and always brief in duration. Compared to the Fourteenth Symphony, there's nothing especially death obsessed about this piece at all, and if the ending sounds mysterious, this is because it's exactly what Shostakovich wanted.

First Movement: Allegretto

Shostakovich described the first movement as taking place in a toy shop, and it's easy to hear why in this collection of skittish and childlike tunes, arranged in sonata form. Solo flute presents the opening theme, followed by a jocular bassoon, with plenty of clicking and crackling commentary from the percussion section. The second subject, beginning as a trumpet solo over an "oompah" accompaniment, is a true summing up of all of those galloplike moments in Shostakovich's previous works that use the rhythm of Rossini's *William Tell* overture, only here he borrows the actual tune too.

Some commentators express puzzlement at this remarkable appearance, so to dispel any possible confusion, it's called a "joke." Music is full of them: even Shostakovich's, but not all are as obvious as this one. The development section continues the homage to Rossini, beginning with a snare-drum roll over which the trumpets offer a distorted version of the trumpet fanfare that immediately precedes that famous gallop. It's a big section, full of incident but easy to follow, as bits of previously heard melody, including *William Tell,* come and go.

You can recognize the arrival of the recapitulation quite clearly after the big cymbal-led climax. The opening melody returns as a duet between piccolo and solo violin, punctuated by quietly rattling percussion. On the way to the second subject, the music becomes positively clownish. Trombones blast out jolly melodies over a jaunty snare-drum rhythm, while the woodwinds interrupt with squeals of approval. It's all good-natured fun. After a last reminder of the *William Tell* overture—this time in the clarinets—flute, piccolo, and glockenspiel whistle and ping the movement to a close, although the last chord for full orchestra comes as a harmonic surprise. This is the kind of music whose freshness and spontaneity could only have come from a composer of vast skill and experience. It is old music that sounds young.

Second Movement: Adagio

No two movements in this symphony share the same form, and this can be viewed as another aspect of its comprehensiveness as a summary of Shostakovich's handling of symphonic construction, for each formal type represented has numerous important predecessors in his work (save for the finale, which is a special case, as you'll see). This adagio is a simple ABA with a short coda based on B. The opening A section follows the same basic pattern as the first subject of the slow movement of the Seventh Symphony: a chorale followed by an instrumental recitative, alternating three times, in diminuendo. In this case, the full brass section provides the chorale and a solo cello the recitative (more shades of the *William Tell* overture, perhaps: its solo cello opening this time).

An eerie interlude consisting of solo cello interrupted by two ghostly dissonant chords—the first on high woodwinds, the second on muted brass—leads to the central B episode. This is a funeral march very, very close to the corresponding sections of the Sixth Symphony's first movement and the First Symphony's lento third movement. It too features instruments in alternation—in this case two flutes, which lead off—and then a very Mahlerian trombone solo with tuba growling beneath. These protagonists toss the funeral march back and forth, until the eerie chord intervenes in a huge crescendo and initiates the movement's climax, at first brilliant and positive, then darkening and turning tragic. Notice the vicious whip cracks, a signature of all of these late works (the first movement had a few as well).

Desolate, tapping rhythms on the woodblock, shades of the third movement of the Thirteenth Symphony and the closing song of the Fourteenth, lead back to the chorale, now on muted strings. Celesta and vibraphone introduce the solo double bass, which now takes over from the solo cello, and in turn leads back to the chorale, first on strings, then as originally on low brass. In the short coda, timpani tap out the funeral-march rhythm while the trombones and tuba quietly emit sharp staccato chords. Suddenly, fortissimo bassoons harmonized in hollow-sounding fifths belch out Shostakovich's DSCH musical monogram (see the discussion of Violin Concerto No. 1 for a further explanation of what exactly this is), and without pause, the scherzo begins.

Third Movement: Allegretto

This movement uses a simple ABAB form, another Shostakovich favorite, particularly in scherzos: witness the First and Sixth Symphonies. The accompaniment in fifths to the main theme of the A section also harks back to the finale of the First Cello Concerto, as does the thematic material itself, which is chromatically spiced, gawky, and inclined to favor the woodwind section. Bits of dance music flit by, very sparingly scored. The B section, on the other hand, introduces lots of mischievous percussion along with a simple motive on solo violin close in tone to the second subject of the Second Violin Concerto's first movement. The "snap, crackle, and pop" percussive interjections, familiar from the first movement, lead eventually to the tick-tock clock music familiar from the Fourth Symphony and Second Cello Concerto.

Divided cellos instead of bassoons now get the DSCH motive and introduce an even more evanescent, sparse recapitulation of the A section, given mostly to solo violin at the start, then to muted trumpets, horns, and trombones, the latter with humorous glissandos tossed in. This reprise is greatly foreshortened, as is that of the B section, which appears in the violins in a tired-sounding, legato variant, before a sprightly solo xylophone, more clock noises, and a couple of cheeps from the piccolo hurry the music to a striking close. The entire movement lasts barely four minutes and seldom rises above a piano dynamic, but it gives the impression of bustling activity all the same, and its puckish wit has little of the heavy-handed grotesquerie of some of Shostakovich's previous scherzos (such as those in the Fifth and Eighth Symphonies).

Finale: Adagio-Allegretto

In addition to working in traditional or simple forms, Shostakovich was equally adept at creating hybrids of his own, and his last symphony fittingly concludes with one of the most remarkable of them. You could describe its nicely symmetrical shape as (AB)C(BA)–coda, except that C is an expansive passacaglia and so has a clear internal structure of its own. This tightly controlled use of form is important, because the movement not only incorporates very wide-ranging material of its own, it refers back to all the other movements as well, and so acts as a genuine summary of the content of the entire work.

The movement opens with a surprise: the "fate" motive from Wagner's *Ring* operas. Shostakovich claimed that this was also derived from a song by Glinka, but aside from the very real possibility that he's playing another joke (despite, or because of, the otherwise dark atmosphere), this motive provides an excellent means of bracketing the movement's form, and its various appearances are, as you will hear, very well placed strategically to clarify the various episodes. After a few reiterations of "fate," complete with Wagner's solo timpani strokes in between, the violins decide they'd rather be playing the prelude to the same composer's *Tristan und Isolde,* but instead of the expected famous chord, the first three Wagnerian notes relax into a wanly beautiful violin melody over a simple pizzicato accompaniment. It's a classic example of that lyrical sweetness so often found in late Shostakovich (think of the finale of the Thirteenth Symphony too), and although it has a tendency to wander, the tune always manages to find its way back to a firm tonal center.

Once this has run its course, a staccato march in the brass introduces the B episode, which, in contrast to the previous melody, is scored almost entirely for woodwinds: flutes, oboes, and clarinets in particular. The strings soon take over, only to have the woodwinds interrupt once again with a lightly skipping figure that sounds like something out of the scherzo. It fades away as "fate" returns on the brass, formally closing this finale's first big section. Over a steady pulsation on the timpani and ominous viola oscillations, the passacaglia (C) now begins, played pizzicato by the cellos and basses. Like the previous examples, the theme has an unusual number of bars (14), but unlike in the Eighth Symphony, the surface activity going on at the same time stays pretty well synchronized with each repetition of the bass line.

Shostakovich does introduce an additional twist, however, in that the passacaglia theme itself exists in two versions: an actual melody, which is how you first hear it, and as a simplified harmonic outline in long notes, which permits the tune to move more freely among the various instrumental voices. There are five repetitions of the melodic version of the theme in pizzicato cellos and basses, over which solo clarinet, then the upper strings (first alone, then with added flute and piccolo) weave pensive webs of sound. The texture brightens for the initial presentation of the long-note version in high violins, celesta, and horn. The theme then migrates back to cellos and basses, bowed this time, still in its alternate form.

A couple of repetitions more allow Shostakovich sufficient time to build the tension in increasingly dense layers of sound, and the climax explodes with a crash on the cymbals: it's the melodic version of the passacaglia theme on trumpets, trombones, tuba, and timpani, with the rest of the orchestra wailing in anguish above and below. As this slowly, painfully, sinks back into the darkness, a crash on the tam-tam and hammering snare drum put an end to the nightmare. Soft strokes on the tam-tam continue to accompany the reprise of the little march tune that introduced B, now played on pizzicato strings, with B itself given to bassoons, then clarinet. The scherzolike skipping figure flits by, and "fate" returns one last time, as a prelude to the final appearance of A's lyrical melody.

This slightly varied version of the tune touches on more major keys than previously, giving the impression of even greater innocence and a definite, if fragile, happiness. As the theme seems to be heading towards a peaceful close, the eerie chord from the second movement interrupts on muted brass. The strings try once again, with the same result. One last effort, and now the chord appears in the high woodwinds, then the strings. Next the passacaglia theme starts in pizzicato cellos and basses, only to be rejected in its turn in exactly the same manner. The celesta then strikes up the opening theme of the first movement: it's a process similar to the one that opens the finale of Beethoven's Ninth, only happening in reverse.

At the sound of the celesta, the strings alight on a sustained fifth, and the entire percussion section enters with the tick-tock music of the third movement. Over this rhythmic pattern, the timpani alternate with the xylophone (plus triangle, celesta, and glockenspiel) in playing bits of the passacaglia theme, coolly impassive, childlike, and purged of any sense of menace. To the rattling sound of a clock that has broken a spring, the percussion rhythm finally skids to a halt as well. All that's left is that open fifth on the strings, slowly fading into silence, unfulfilled, when suddenly celesta, triangle, and glockenspiel toss in the missing note of the major chord. And so the last symphony of Shostakovich ends, neither with a bang nor a whimper but with a sly wink and a smile. Who could have guessed that it would turn out this way?

Postlude

In considering Shostakovich's work, the listener effectively has two choices: focus on contingent circumstances, the speculative relationship between art and life, and therefore on what might have been; or in the alternative, concentrate on what is, on what Shostakovich actually did and why it should matter today. If his music survives, then the universal emotions that it expresses must inevitably appear to be more significant than the hidden messages it also contains. Indeed, the more familiar his output becomes, the more likely it seems that the secret meaning of Shostakovich's oeuvre as a whole is his desire, as he expressed to Flora Litvinova at the time of the Fourteenth Symphony, to create pure music, to drop the mask and be free to write as he pleased. In other words, the true subtext is his music's validity as music, plain and simple.

The evidence supports this. If you look at the "Summary of Individual Movement Forms" (appendix 2), you will notice that among the twenty-one works discussed here, no two adopt the same large-scale structure. That cannot be an accident. Also, no two of Shostakovich's string quartets share the same key. Add in the interesting formal correspondences between Symphonies Nos. 8–11 and the similarly numbered quartets, and you can make a very good case for an extremely self-conscious effort on Shostakovich's part to give each new composition its special place in a larger framework, one created and defined by musical considerations alone. Naturally this isn't as interesting as saying "He wrote this as a protest against Stalinism," but the truth is that one conception doesn't preclude the other. Both may well be true, and my only suggestion is that at this late date, it's time to look more closely at this remarkably coherent body of work and try to see how the musical pieces of the puzzle fit together, because any sensible listener hears them clearly.

Shostakovich began his career with a musical gift of Mozartian proportions, and he died at age sixty-nine, at the height of his powers. The emphasis on death and mortality that we hear spoken of so often in connection with his last period tends to make us forget that he was not, in fact, all that old at the time of his passing. And if it's true that he was thinking of his works in terms of larger musical cycles, then he was hardly finished. He even said as much on more than one occasion. It certainly looks as though he was planning twenty-four string quartets, one in each major and minor key, like the 24 Preludes and Fugues, Op. 87, for piano. But he only finished fifteen of them. The symphonies are a messier bunch, because he started them so much earlier and the stylistic variety on offer is correspondingly wider, but there is no reason to assume that the Fifteenth would have been the last in that series of works either. And can it be a coincidence that there are two concertos for each of piano, violin, and cello? Or fifteen symphonies and fifteen quartets?

So although it's convenient to speak of "late" Shostakovich, and however conscious of his own closeness to death he must have been towards the end, there is no need to subscribe to the romantic notion of the dying artist composing, over and over, his own requiem. This is the view fostered to some degree in *Testimony,* and however valuable that book otherwise remains, in this respect it strikes me as nonsense. The music says otherwise. If Shostakovich did write his own epitaph, then you can find it in the finale of his last major orchestral work, the starkly magnificent *Suite on Verses by Michelangelo Buonarroti*. There, to a tune written when he was still a youngster and used so many years later, he set the following beautiful text:

Immortality

Here fate has sent eternal sleep to me,
But although buried in the earth, I am not dead:
I live within you, whose laments I heed,
Because we are reflections of each other.

I seem as one dead, but as consolation to the world,
I still live in the hearts, and in the thousands of souls, of all loving people,
And this means that I am not dust,
And mortal decay does not touch me.

The ending of this work, like that of the Fourth, Eighth, and Fifteenth Symphonies, as well as the Second Cello Concerto, gazes unflinchingly out into infinity. For all that Shostakovich may have suffered, and despite the fact that he claimed not to take any solace from religion, his is not in the final analysis a pessimistic view. In this very poem, he reaches back across the centuries and makes contact with another artist, a man of a very different time and place, and knows that he is not alone. That is the power of art, and of Shostakovich's music. His spirit lives within it—decent, humane, honest, troubled, sarcastic, angry, tormented, joyous, tragic, funny, and compassionate—just as he lives within us as we listen. These pieces may not always speak of hope, and their victories may not always ring true, but isn't that what happens sometimes in life? And all of Shostakovich's music, every note, is about life.

Appendix 1: Chronology of Works

Although not absolutely complete, the following list includes most of Shostakovich's major works, and more than a few minor ones, arranged in strict chronological order. I have largely omitted the numerous suites drawn from the ballets and the film scores, as their presence tends to obscure Shostakovich's stylistic evolution by inserting various arrangements of earlier works amid the later pieces. Most published lists that I have seen either proceed strictly by opus number, thus producing a confusingly mixed chronology, or divide up the various works by genre. In contrast, what I offer here will better enable you to use the works discussed in detail in this book as springboards to a wider listening experience, including the music written in close proximity to them.

Theme and Variations, Op. 3, for orchestra (1922)
Piano Trio No. 1 (1923)
Symphony No. 1 (1924–25)
Piano Sonata No. 1 (1926)
Symphony No. 2 (1927)
The Nose (opera) (1927–28)
Tahiti Trot (arrangement of V. Youmans's "Tea for Two") (1928)
New Babylon (film score) (1928–29)
Six Songs to Japanese Poets (1928–32)
Symphony No. 3 (1929)

The Flea (incidental music) (1929)
The Golden Age (ballet) (1930)
The Bolt (ballet) (1930-1)
Alone (film score) (1931)
Hypothetically Murdered (incidental music) (1931)
Golden Hills (film score) (1931)
Rule, Britannia (incidental music) (1931)
Hamlet (incidental music) (1931-2)
Lady Macbeth of Mtsensk District (opera) (1930-2)
Passer-by (film score) (1932)
The Counterplan (film score) (1932)
24 Preludes for Piano (1932–33)
Piano Concerto No. 1 (1933)
The Human Comedy (incidental music) (1934)
Cello Sonata (1934)
Suite for Jazz Orchestra (1934)
Love and Hate (film score) (1934)
The Limpid Stream (ballet) (1934–35)
The Youth of Maxim (film score) (1934–35)
Girl Friends (film score) (1934–35)
String Quartet No. 1 (1935)
Symphony No. 4 (1935–36)
Four Pushkin Romances (1936)
The Tale of the Priest and his Servant Balda (animated film score) (1936)
Golden Mountains (film score) (1936)
The Return of Maxim (film score) (1936–37)
Volochayev Days (film score) (1937)
Symphony No. 5 (1937)
Friends (film score) (1938)
Vyborg District (film score: Maxim Trilogy No. 3) (1938)
Suite for Theater Orchestra (Jazz Suite No. 2) (1938)
The Man with the Gun (film score) (1938)

Chronology of Works

A Great Citizen I and II (film scores) (1938–39)
Symphony No. 6 (1939)
The Tale of the Silly Little Mouse (animated film score) (1939)
King Lear (incidental music) (1940)
Piano Quintet (1940)
Mussorgsky: *Boris Godunov* (reorchestration of opera) (1940)
The Adventures of Korzinkina (film score) (1940)
Symphony No. 7 (1941)
Six Songs by Raleigh, Burns and Shakespeare (1942)
Piano Sonata No. 2 (1942)
Symphony No. 8 (1943)
Zoya (film score) (1944)
Piano Trio No. 2 (1944)
String Quartet No. 2 (1944)
Eight English and American Folksongs (1944)
Symphony No. 9 (1945)
String Quartet No. 3 (1946)
Pirogov (film score) (1947)
Poem on the Homeland (cantata) (1947)
Violin Concerto No. 1 (1947–48; revised 1955)
The Young Guard (film score) (1947-8)
Michurin (film score) (1948)
From Jewish Folk Poetry (song cycle) (1948)
Encounter at the Elbe (film score) (1948)
Rayok ("Little Paradise") (cantata) (1948)
String Quartet No. 4 (1949)
The Fall of Berlin (film score) (1949)
The Song of the Forests (oratorio) (1949)
Belinsky (film score) (1950)
24 Preludes and Fugues for Piano (1950–51)
The Unforgettable Year—1919 (film score) (1951)
Ten Poems on Verses by Revolutionary Poets (for unaccompanied chorus) (1951)

Four Pushkin Monologues (song cycle) (1952)
The Sun Shines on Our Motherland (cantata) (1952)
String Quartet No. 5 (1952)
Concertino for Two Pianos (1953)
Symphony No. 10 (1953)
Festive Overture (1954)
Song of the Great Rivers (*Unity*) (film score) (1954)
The Gadfly (film score) (1955)
String Quartet No. 6 (1956)
Simple People (film score) (1956)
The First Echelon (film score) (1956)
Piano Concerto No. 2 (1957)
Symphony No. 11 (1957)
Moskva Cheremushki (musical comedy) (1959)
Mussorgsky: *Khovanshchina* (orchestration of opera) (1959)
Cello Concerto No. 1 (1959)
String Quartet No. 7 (1960)
String Quartet No. 8 (1960)
Five Days—Five Nights (film score) (1960)
Satires (song cycle) (1960)
Symphony No. 12 (1961)
Symphony No. 13 (1962)
The Young Lady and the Hooligan (ballet adapted by L. Atovmian) (1962)
Mussorgsky: *Songs and Dances of Death* (orchestration of song cycle) (1962)
Overture on Russian and Kirghiz Folk Themes (1963)
The Execution of Stepan Razin (cantata) (1964)
Hamlet (film score) (1964)
String Quartet No. 9 (1964)
String Quartet No. 10 (1964)
A Year is Like a Lifetime (film score) (1965)
Cello Concerto No. 2 (1966)

Chronology of Works

String Quartet No. 11 (1966)
October (symphonic poem) (1967)
Sofia Perovskaya (film score) (1967)
Violin Concerto No. 2 (1967)
Seven Blok Songs (1967)
String Quartet No. 12 (1968)
Violin Sonata (1968)
Symphony No. 14 (1969)
King Lear (film score) (1970)
String Quartet No. 13 (1970)
Faithfulness (8 ballads for male chorus) (1970)
Symphony No. 15 (1971)
Six Songs by Marina Tsvetayeva (1973)
String Quartet No. 14 (1973)
Suite on Verses by Michelangelo Buonarroti (song cycle) (1974)
String Quartet No. 15 (1974)
Four Verses by Captain Lebyadkin (song cycle) (1975)
Viola Sonata (1975)

Appendix 2: Summary of Individual Movement Forms

Work	Movement 1	2	3	4	5
Symphony No. 1 (3 + 4 linked)	Sonata Allegro	ABAB	ABAB*	Sonata Allegro	
Symphony No. 2 (w/ closing chorus)	Free Form				
Symphony No. 3 (w/ closing chorus)	Free Form				
Symphony No. 4	ABABA	ABABA	ABABA		
Symphony No. 5	Slow Sonata	ABA	Slow Sonata*	Sonata Allegro	
Symphony No. 6	ABAB*	ABAB	ABAB		
Symphony No. 7 (3 + 4 linked)	Sonata Allegro	Rondo	Slow Sonata	ABA	
Symphony No. 8 (3–5 linked)	Slow Sonata	Sonata Allegro	Toccata (ABA)	Passacaglia*	Sonata-Rondo
Symphony No. 9 (3–5 linked)	Sonata Allegro	ABABA*	ABA	ABAB*	Sonata Allegro
Symphony No. 10	Slow Sonata	ABA	Sonata-Rondo*	Sonata Allegro	
Symphony No. 11 (plays continuously)	ABABCBA*	(DE)AFAEAB	GHEG*	(IE)D(AE)DE	
Symphony No. 12 (plays continuously)	Sonata Allegro	ABA*	Free Form	Rondo	
Symphony No. 13 (all vocal: 3–5 linked)	Slow Sonata	Rondo	ABABABA*	ABACDAEA*	Rondo
Symphony No. 14 (all vocal: 11 songs)	S	FFS	FSS	FS	SF
Symphony No. 15 (2 + 3 linked)	Sonata Allegro	ABA*	ABAB	AB–Passacaglia–BA	
Violin Concerto No. 1 (3–5 linked)	Variations*	Sonata Allegro	Passacaglia*	Cadenza	Rondo
Violin Concerto No. 2 (2 + 3 linked)	Slow Sonata	ABA*	Rondo		
Cello Concerto No. 1 (2–4 linked)	Sonata Allegro	Sonata-Rondo*	Cadenza	Rondo	
Cello Concerto No. 2 (2 + 3 linked)	Slow Sonata	Sonata Allegro	Variations		
Piano Concerto No. 1 (2–4 linked)	Sonata-Rondo	ABA*	Free Form	Rondo	
Piano Concerto No. 2 (2 + 3 linked)	Sonata Allegro	ABABA*	Sonata Allegro		

* = slow movement (where not otherwise indicated); F = fast; S = slow

Selected Bibliography

The Shostakovich biographical literature is large and contentious. The following four books offer a reasonably complete overview of the range of material available to the interested listener:

Galina: A Russian Story. Galina Vishnevskaya. Harcourt Brace Jovanovich, 1984.

While not strictly about Shostakovich, this autobiography of one of his closest collaborators, Russia's greatest soprano during the Soviet era, contains so much useful information about artistic life in general, and is so much fun to read in its own right, that it offers an ideal place to start.

Shostakovich: A Life Remembered. Elizabeth Wilson. Princeton University Press, 1994.

This excellent collection of personal reminisces of the composer offers many different perspectives. Naturally the commentaries are colored by the vagaries of memory and the personal agendas of each contributor, but what emerges is a vivid and fascinating eyewitness portrait of a complex, brilliant, witty, sarcastic, kind, decent, and often tormented soul.

Testimony: The Memoirs of Dmitri Shostakovich. Solomon Volkov. Limelight Editions, 1979.

Controversy still swirls around this book, which created a sensation on its original publication. Among the questions: How much time did Volkov actually spend with the composer? How accurate is his transmittal of what he was allegedly told? How faithful to the composer's intentions (if any) is the final version of the text? In its basics, the tale that the composer allegedly tells has been confirmed by his friends and family, but then, many of the facts are not in doubt. It is the unrelieved bitterness and the degree to which Shostakovich was self-consciously an artist/dissident that continues to raise scholarly eyebrows. Read, and judge for yourself.

Shostakovich: A Life. Laurel E. Fay. Oxford University Press, 2000.

At the opposite pole from Volkov stands this excellently researched book by Laurel Fay. What she has done is simply examine the archival evidence in order to see if the mythology promulgated by the Shostakovich circle has some basis in written fact. Of course, the accuracy of Soviet documents is in itself a source of controversy, and by downplaying the significance of oral history and other kinds of evidence, Fay has opened herself up to some virulent attacks. But what emerges from this study—a frank assessment of an artist struggling to cope and making the terrible compromises necessary to preserve his dignity, his ideals, and ultimately his life—is in some ways more believable than Volkov's portrait.

CD Track Listing

Symphony No. 5, Op. 45

1. Moderato (15:14)
2. Allegretto (5:29)
3. Largo (13:55)
4. Allegro non troppo (10:48)

The Stockholm Philharmonic Orchestra
Yuri Ahronovitch, Conductor
BIS-CD-357
© 1986 and 1987, BIS Records AB

Recordings licensed under permission of BIS Records AB. All rights reserved.